Advance praise for *Hire Your Buyer*

I strongly recommend *Hire Your Buyer* to entrepreneurs, lawyers, accountants, tax practitioners, estate planning consultants and wealth managers. This informative and entertaining book identifies many of the complex issues in transitioning ownership or control of the family business... *Hire Your Buyer* is definitely a must-read!
—*Richard M. Wise, FCPA, FCA, FCBV, FASA, C. Arb.*
Partner, Valuation Group, MNP, LLP
Lead Author, Guide to Canadian Business Valuations

This is an important contribution to the business owner/business transition literature... well done!
—*Tom Deans, PhD, Award-Winning Speaker, Bestselling Author*

With keen insight that comes from substantial experience, John Mill goes deep into the hard and soft issues of business transition. Beyond this incisive analysis, he provides innovative real-world solutions to some of the most vexing problems owners face as they look to capture the full value of their life's work.
—*Matthew Wesley, Founder and Family Advisor, The Wesley Group*

John Mill has provided a thorough, well-researched path to growing value in your business, setting yourself up for long-term success. I highly recommend this book: It will change the way you think about your business.
—*Jason R. Watt, CD, CLU, RHU, Instructor and Owner, Business Career College Corp.*

In *Hire Your Buyer*, John has taken a complex topic and clarified the issues for everyone to understand. He examines legal and financial considerations alongside the human emotions that all interplay. Well done!
—*Liz Robertson, Executive Director, Canadian Association of Farm Advisors*

A *must* read for all business owners in all types of businesses, large or small. John's easy-to-read style, depth of research and case studies illustrate to business owners the pitfalls to avoid and the most successful strategies to embrace to empower them, their families and the future of their business.
—*Barry Mills, CPCA, Vanrooy, Mills & Associates, Succession, Exit and Retirement Strategist*

John Mill *really* understands the small business market. He understands how quickly M&A transactions can spell a company's doom if they are not conceived and executed sensibly. This is the classic guide to mergers and acquisitions, offering practical advice for keeping deals on track and ensuring post-closing integration success. He has done a great thing for small and medium-sized business professionals.
—*Mark Borkowski, President, Mercantile Mergers & Acquisitions Corp.*

As a professional and business owner who has worked on both sides of the table, this book is a must read!
—*Scott M. Rasenberg, CPA, CA, VP Finance, JMR Electric Ltd., former tax partner at a national accounting firm*

I couldn't put the book down! Though short in format, it is packed with great insight into the elements that affect the sale of a business. Those who follow the author's philosophy will profit greatly from his advice.
—*Arthur Dolan, Professional Facilitator, Dolan Estate Settlement Services Inc.*

John has a keen ability to instruct and entertain at the same time. The topic – maximizing value in the transition of a small business – is often overlooked and well worthy of his keen insight.
—*Derek van der Plaat, Managing Director, Veracap M&A International Inc.*

Hire Your Buyer

HIRE YOUR BUYER!

A Philosophy of Value Creation

John Mill

Engagement Thinking Tools Co.

Published and distributed by

Engagement Thinking Tools Co.
180–13300 Tecumseh Rd. E.
Tecumseh, Ontario   N8N 4R8

Although the author has exhaustively researched all sources to ensure the accuracy and completeness of the information contained in this book, we assume no responsibility for errors, inaccuracies, omissions or inconsistencies herein. Any slights of people or organizations are unintentional. Readers should use their own judgment and/or consult a financial and legal expert for specific applications to their individual situations.

Most of the stories featured in this book are based on real events. Except in reports of legal cases where the facts are a matter of public record, names and other identifying details have been changed to protect privacy.

ISBN 978-0-9938431-0-5

Editor: Donna Dawson, CPE
Cover design: The Branding Experts
Interior layout and design: Iva Cheung

To order more copies of *Hire Your Buyer*, visit www.hireyourbuyer.com.

To my boys, whom I love and who inspire me.

Acknowledgments

Thanks to Tripp Braden for introducing me to *The Terrible Truth about Lawyers*, Matt Wesley for *The Moral Imagination* and "How Wolves Change Rivers," Chrissy Guthoerl for introducing me to *Good to Great*, Nereo Bagatto for the phrase "skill in the game," Barry Mills for the phrase "slow-down plan," Kevin Ballantyne for introducing me to the CoreValue Software, and Ken Sanginario and Michael Corrigan for explaining the Value Opportunity Profile.

Thank you to Richard Wise, author of the three-volume *Guide to Canadian Business Valuations,* for helping me to explain some of the more complicated valuation concepts, and to Jason Kwiatkowski, chartered business valuator, for suggesting that zero multiple is a multiple. Thanks to Chris Delaney for hours of discussion and for producing a foreword in record time. Thanks also to Tom Deans, bestselling author, for his advice and encouragement.

I would like to acknowledge my readability editor, Kerri Dunwoody, and my professional editor, Donna Dawson. Thanks also to Iva Cheung for book layout and Ed Roach of the Branding Experts for many long hours of discussion and revision of the images for the book.

I also had a team of 55 reviewers, many of whom read the book and provided valuable feedback and in some cases testimonials.

Contents

Foreword

THREE YEARS AGO, I was working with several families on their estate, tax and business succession planning needs. As a lawyer, these were typical consulting engagements for me: a deep discovery process resulted in several efficiency suggestions, which I proffered for consideration and implementation by the clients' own professional advisor teams (lawyers and accountants). In most cases, at least two or three of the suggestions were readily apparent; they tended to be driven by tax savings.

At the conclusion of each of three separate client meetings in less than a month, I was asked versions of a profound and unusual question: "These suggestions are fabulous and will save us a lot of tax and expense – but how do we get this wealth to our family?"

It was an epiphany for me and forced a great deal of self-reflection. I had always striven to provide suggestions and insights with a view to making clients advocates for their own planning. I understood many years ago that a disengaged client typically received a listless and pedestrian outcome. These clients were now asking a deeper and more profound question that drove to the very heart of a purposeful wealth transfer plan. They were expressing a yearning for directions to and then guidance on a path of sustainable intergenerational relationships between their wealth and their family. They wanted to understand a different way to engage with their life's work.

In response to those questions, I began searching for resources and collaborators to help me in my own journey to be a better, more thoughtful family wealth advisor. On that path, I have had the great pleasure of meeting and working with John Mill, the author of *Hire Your Buyer*. From 2012 to 2014 we spent countless hours over coffee in London, Ontario, and Denver, Colorado, discussing purposeful planning and, ultimately, the elements of this book. John was traveling along his own path of professional discovery.

In *Hire Your Buyer* you will experience the results of that odyssey. John has created a resource that incorporates an inherently purposeful approach and has woven that sinew into the structure of a business value creation model. The result is a profoundly different approach to business succession that will be appropriate for some business owners and that adds another arrow to the planning quiver for transition specialists.

Every business will undergo transition. But the statistics on sustaining wealth between generations or sale parties are frightening: 70% of wealth doesn't survive beyond the successor's hands. In many cases, the transition of a business is the start of a significant wealth destruction phase for a family. This destruction can ravage families and relationships for years beyond the transition date.

Fear of that devastation was what underpinned my clients asking how they could get the wealth to their families. What they really meant was, "How do we transfer and sustain that wealth in a meaningful, healthy and purposeful manner?" That is a fundamentally different starting point than is typically used.

Many business succession resources exist. They are often associated with tax strategies or valuation principles. These are useful and important concepts and cannot be ignored. Taxation is a significant threat to value for most business owners. Understanding the value of your business provides realistic metrics for timing and enjoying your retirement. Thoughtful and collaborative multidisciplinary advice is essential to understanding the complexity of the succession process.

As John's work implies, however, business succession isn't just tax and it isn't just valuation – it's a much richer and more complex tapestry. It's a process that requires purpose, vision, strategy, values, innovation and culture. The hire your buyer strategy incorporates these values into the very fabric of the business itself to allow, if appropriate, for an internal acquisition by employees. Done right, the strategy creates an engine of sustainable value growth.

I would add that if done properly, the hire your buyer approach is also a business process that will infuse the family with purpose, vision, values and personal innovation, creating a family wealth strategy and a sustainable intergenerational culture. In this respect, a hire your buyer strategy becomes a win-win proposition for the sellers and the buyers and substantially answers that critical question: "How *do* we get this wealth to our family?"

Chris Delaney
Family Wealth Strategist,
Business Succession Advisor, Speaker and Author

Introduction

THIS IS A BOOK for people who like to read. Wherever possible the points in the book are made through stories and examples; technical material is kept to a minimum. It is written primarily for small business owners, but the value creation ideas are universal and apply to any business.

What Is Hiring Your Buyer?

This book offers a solution to a substantial crisis facing business owners between the ages of 50 and 70. In the United States there are six million of these owners and in Canada there are 550,000. It is estimated that 55% of these businesses will transfer or disappear as a result of a calamity. The ensuing fiscal carnage will be a threat to the entire economy.

Many small business owners operate in a blissful state, assuming they can always sell their businesses. But the average price of a business listed on the largest business sale website in the US is $155,000, and that's not going to cut it. It comes as quite a surprise to many owners that the same business that pays them $200,000 a year may have zero transfer value. Further, some estimates say that only 30% of businesses go to family members. That leaves millions of businesses in the danger zone.

Aside from selling, business owners have only a few other options. You may be able to take your business public or sell your app to a high-tech firm, but for most of us that won't work. The most readily available option for those with a solid business foundation and the right team-building skills is to hire your buyer. That is, work with the people in your business; form a team; strategize; clarify your purpose, vision and values; and build more value in your business. Train your successor or team of successors and then watch your business flourish and share in the value created as you transfer it to the new ownership team. That's hiring your buyer.

The actual buyer, or team of buyers, may be existing employees or one or more of your children, or you may have to go out and find them. If you are an owner you need to decide whether this option is for you and if it is, you need to take the active steps to make it happen. This book shows you how.

The Second E-Myth

Over 25 years ago, Michael E. Gerber wrote a bestselling business book called *The E-Myth: Why Most Businesses Don't Work and What to Do about It*. The e-myth (that is, the entrepreneur myth) is the mistaken belief that most businesses are started by people with tangible business skills, when in fact most are started by "technicians" who know nothing about running a business. Hence, most fail.

By contrast, consider that almost every business owner between 50 and 70 is one of the 20% who survived the cut. And most are successful entrepreneurs supporting a decent lifestyle. There are millions of owners who have spent decades building a *solid business foundation*. This is significant; it means something. Creating a solid business foundation is the most difficult stage of a business. The site has been excavated, the forms put in, the concrete poured and set. But then what happens? For most of these owners, the answer is nothing – they stop building the business at the foundation stage. Why? Because the business satisfies their lifestyle needs.

But there is a *second* e-myth, one that Gerber did not talk about. Most entrepreneurs believe *they are creating value in their business*. This is a myth. A business is something separate from the owner; a business is something that has value and can be sold. What most entrepreneurs have created is a lucrative, interesting job for themselves, but not a business with significant value that they can sell.

These entrepreneurs are lifestyle business owners. Their businesses are designed to be the foundation of a decent lifestyle, to generate a good salary and to serve as a vehicle for freedom and expression. The problem is that there is no way that selling that business will support a decent lifestyle in retirement.

· · · · · · · · · · · · · ·

*Most entrepreneurs believe they are creating value in their business. **This is a myth.***

· · · · · · · · · · · · · ·

These businesses are not professionally managed – the entrepreneur covers almost all management functions and makes all the decisions. And these decisions are made for the convenience and comfort of the owner, not for the purpose of maximizing the value of the business. Combine this lifestyle business behavior with the fact that 90% of owners have done no succession planning and suddenly you realize that this crisis *is an opportunity*. The opportunity is that there are millions of solid business foundations that have never been built up to their full potential.

The opportunity lies in building up that solid business foundation and creating a second and third floor of value that everyone can share. These solid business foundations are the secret sauce that will allow the hire your buyer formula – employee engagement and share ownership – to work.

OK, sounds easy. Why isn't everyone doing it?

That's what I wondered, so I tried to figure it out. This book is the result. The reason everyone isn't doing it is that they don't know how. What's more, a lot of trusted advisors tell owners they should not give employees share ownership because

- » Employees who own shares have a right to see financial statements
- » Employees have to have "skin in the game" (a sizable down payment)
- » Most of them just can't afford it
- » You can't get your money on closing
- » You can't trust employees to run a business – they are not entrepreneurs

The other big argument you will hear from business valuators is that you will get a better price for your business from a strategic or synergistic purchaser. These buyers can pay a lot more because they get more value by strategically combining your business with their own and creating synergies. Business valuators say that if employees buy the business there are no new synergies because nothing changes; they won't be able to save a lot of money by firing a bunch of redundant employees when they take over.

This has not been my experience. Sharing financial information – when you are prepared to share the rewards – does not cause problems, it solves them. If you want to build a second or third floor of value on a business foundation then *skill* in the game is much more important than *skin* in the game. And if you do build that second and third floor of value there will be plenty of money to go around.

I do agree that if you can sell to a strategic purchaser and satisfy your goals, you should. But endlessly clinging to the hope that someday you will be saved by a strategic purchaser – when you can't sell your business today – is a recipe for disaster. This book shows you how *strategic growth* blows the doors off *strategic purchaser* any day.

Why I Am Qualified to Write This Book

Why me? I am well suited to this task. I started my career as an entrepreneur and then I went back to law school to become a small business lawyer. I have worked on every aspect of small business legal issues and I obtained a master's degree in tax law along the way. I have appeared in the Canadian Federal Court of Appeal and I have coordinated large teams of professionals in both trials and transactions. Because of my roots as an entrepreneur I have always searched for value in whatever I have done. I have always kept searching and poking into things, ever hopeful that the rainbow would reveal the pot of gold – and it finally has.

What I Learned about Value Creation Surprised Me

What I learned in writing and researching this book surprised me. After 30 years of searching for value creation ideas I finally found a very simple, straightforward concept that anyone can use. It is not technical tax planning or sophisticated legal structures that create significant value. Instead it is the quality of the relationships among the people involved in the business that creates value. I learned that *engagement* and *trust* are the keys to value creation.

What is engagement?

Engagement is an excited, interested curiosity to see what's next and to be part of the process. Engagement arises out of having enough information about your environment to make choices that create value in that environment.

When you hire your buyer you have to give up the traditional legal notions of control and direction. You have to engage. You have to trust. This is not a naive trust, this is a sophisticated trust. It is a trust built on a two-way street. That street is called *freedom and responsibility*. The freedom you give your buyer has to be matched by the level of responsibility the buyer exercises. It is the same as the idea that the founding fathers used to engage citizens to build a great country.

But where do you learn about the idea of engagement? To learn you have to find out who has experimented and studied it a lot. Employee engagement is a significant topic in the field of business management and human relations at many Fortune 500 companies.

To learn more about engagement I had to learn more about management and for that reason there are a lot of management stories in the book. When I tell Google's management story it is only to point out that even those on Mount Olympus who look down on us mortals have realized that the key to value creation in their own business lies in the simple virtues of good human relationships.

And as the founding father or mother of your own business, if you want to build a culture of freedom and responsibility, you have to treat people well and then get out of the way. And if you think about it, that works out quite well for someone who is looking to slow down and build value at the same time.

Value Creation Is Not Rocket Science. In Fact, It's Not Science at All

The central question in business succession planning is, how do we create enough value to satisfy everyone's needs? When you hire your buyer you are adding mouths to feed. A value gap occurs when you do not have enough value both inside and outside your business to finance your retirement lifestyle. If you have a value gap then simply adding people to your business makes it worse. This means that to make the hire your buyer formula work, it is essential to understand value creation.

Value creation is a human endeavor that cannot be reduced to a formula or an equation. Business owners need a set of principles – a philosophy, a disciplined way of thinking – that guides decision-making. The type of value creation explained in this book is *strategic growth*. A concern among many of the risk-averse professionals who will read this book is that there is no real science to prove *with certainty* that value creation works. In other words, there is a risk that no value will be created, that the second and third floor will not be built. This is why I turned to philosophy.

Philosophy, or intelligent speculation, provided the first formative steps of all the sciences. Science is based on proof. As soon as testing can produce certainty, the subject ceases to be philosophy and becomes science. The study of the heavens, which now belongs to astronomy, was once included in philosophy.

Value creation is still a philosophical exercise. There is no testing that can prove with certainty that a hire your buyer plan will work. Other important philosophical topics we will discuss are leadership and management.

Lack of proof has not stopped others from embracing these ideas. Psychologist Abraham Maslow was fascinated with the subject of management. He was impressed that management theorists had come to many of the same conclusions about human nature that psychologists had. The workplace is an important part of the life of a self-actualized person and Maslow speculated that a fully self-actualized *workplace* could accomplish great things.

Because these areas are still philosophical they're rife with uncertainty. Most professionals are uncomfortable with uncertainty and dismiss ideas that cannot be proven with scientific certainty. Consider accountants. Their core discipline is auditing and it infuses their entire approach to everything they deal with. In an audit, if you can't prove an expense with certainty, it doesn't exist.

As a trial lawyer I had different training. In court lawyers have to prove their cases on the balance of probabilities. This balance is symbolized by the blindfolded Goddess of Justice holding the scales. To win you just have to tip the scales. The goal is 51%, not scientific certainty. As a trial lawyer, I'm comfortable with the philosophy of management consultants. I like Maslow's theory of self-actualized organizations and it seems obvious that win-win is better than win-lose. Most importantly I believe – with certainty – that strategic growth will work for a lot of owners.

Engagement is not a mystical secret ritual; engagement is based on ordinary commonsense behavior that anyone can learn. You don't have to be a big company to be a great company.

. . . .

The central question in business succession planning is, how do we create enough value to satisfy everyone's needs?

. . . .

What's the secret? Simple, really. Do you like people? Do you like to see them succeed? Could you coach an under-11 team and get the kids excited about playing even after a disappointing loss? If so, you can create value. If you can create value, you'll be able to hire your buyer.

This book sets out a philosophy of win-win thinking, employee engagement, value creation and leadership. Operating together as part of an intelligent design, these elements bring value into existence. This philosophy has conquered many industries, and it can help a lot of us small business folk get to a better place in our lives.

What's in This Book?

I spent two years organizing this book. I read more than 100 books and at least 1,000 blog posts and articles, looking for commonalities, patterns and evidence. The result is a series of stories woven together to form a framework and set out a comprehensive process for approaching the task of hiring and engaging your buyer or team of buyers. Here's what you'll find:

Chapter 1, The State of Business Succession. We start with the stories of succession failure – the way succession normally happens. We also look into the reasons lifestyle businesses have so little transfer value.

HIRE YOUR BUYER

SHARE

TEAM BUILDS VALUE

SOLID BUSINESS FOUNDATION

Chapter 2, Can I Sell My Business? The Value Gap. In this chapter we review the steps required if you want to sell your business, how to determine whether you can and how to determine whether you can get enough money out of your business sale to retire.

Chapter 3, Value Quicksand: I'm Great, You're Not. The entrepreneurial attitude that "I'm great, you're not" prevents owners from being able to hire a buyer and work as a team to create value. To solve these problems, owners and advisors have to grow internally and conquer the inner demons holding them back.

Chapter 4, The Search for Value: Lessons from the World's Best. Have you ever thought there has to be a better way? There is – and if you want to hire your buyer and build value you need to develop these skills. The evidence points conclusively in the direction of trust and win-win behaviors.

Chapter 5, The Martial Art of Win-Win: Mastering Soft Skills. When you build a team you have to trust them. But we are not talking about a naive, inexperienced type of trust. We are talking about a superior set of skills that will allow you to set the value creation stage.

Chapter 6, Value Creation: Strategic Growth. The chapter confronts the reality that most small businesses do not create value. For a hire your buyer plan to succeed you have to create value. This chapter shows you how.

Chapter 7, Employee Engagement: We're Great. Now that you know how value is created you have to build a team dedicated to creating that value. The key is employee engagement. This chapter talks about how to engage employees and build a winning team.

Chapter 8, Entrepreneur Engagement: Leadership. Have you ever thought about how to win? Here we speak directly to the change the entrepreneur must make to engage the team of buyers and lead the process of value creation.

Chapter 9, A Different Ending. Here I retell one of the stories from the beginning of the book but this time our owner, instead of walking onto quicksand, hires a buyer and emerges as the hero.

Appendix: Seven Steps for Determining Business Value. This simple tool will help you determine the transfer value for your business and from there you can decide whether you have a value gap.

Definitions: Exit, Succession or Riding It Out?

Before we go any further, let me take a minute to make sure we're all on the same page by providing a few basic definitions of terms I'll be using throughout the book.

Exit planning is preparing the business for sale, meaning it can be sold for a price the owner wants. Exit planning involves the short-term sprucing up of the business, getting ready for due diligence and maximizing the enterprise value that can be realized.

Succession is the process of passing something, like your business, to another person or a group of people.

Transition has a wider meaning than succession and refers to the entire life event and all the circumstances both in and out of the business that go along with succession.

Management succession is a human resources term. It refers to the planned hiring, training and replacement of company executives. In large companies the board of directors is responsible for hiring the successor CEO and senior managers.

Business succession means the transfer of the business ownership to successors. There may also be management succession, depending on the management currently in place. The transfer can take anywhere from two to 20 years, depending on the needs of the owner. The successor could be an employee, a child of the owner or an external person. The founding owner may stay involved for a few years of training and business development and perhaps even a few decades in a reduced capacity – the slow-down plan.

Riding it out – or milking it – is what happens when the owner just does not want to leave. This was not such an issue 50 years ago, when most people had a short retirement. But the problem has become much worse as a result of steadily increasing lifespans. Many people now live for dozens of years after they are no longer capable of running a vigorous business.

Chapter 1

The State of Business Succession

I'D LIKE TO BEGIN by telling you an unnecessarily sad story that reveals what can happen in an average, ordinary, reasonably successful business if succession planning – and all that entails – is ignored. By the end of the book it will be very clear how you can avoid this outcome.

Jack Martin: Machine Shop Owner

Jack Martin turned 68 in 2006 (details have been changed); he had owned Martin Machining Inc. (MarMac) for 33 years. Jack was a gruff old-school type who didn't display affection or talk too much. When they were growing up, his children rarely saw him because he was always at the shop and when they did see him he was exhausted.

Twenty years earlier Jack had asked his oldest son, Fred, to come in and learn the business. Fred had tried but he made some mistakes. Fred had some ideas about playing guitar in a band. Jack disapproved; he always said that Fred should learn a trade. Jack was critical and was reluctant to give Fred responsibility until he was ready.

Angela Barrister, a licensed insurance broker, told Jack that it was very risky to have all his investments in one basket – the business. Angela explained that a private pension plan for Jack and his wife would provide security. She thought 5% was a pretty good return for a pension. Jack replied that his own business was his best investment.

Jack preferred dealing with his lawyers and accountants. They agreed that Angela was a decent sort but felt she was really just a sales rep who didn't understand business. "Why pay commissions and fees for investments at 5% when you could get much better returns in your own company?"

In 2006 MarMac's best sales rep, Emilio Santarosa, told Jack he had received a good offer from a competitor, QuantaTool. Emilio's wife was pregnant so he preferred to stay at MarMac rather than take a risk on an offer from QuantaTool that might not work out. Emilio wanted to buy some shares and maybe someday take over MarMac, since Jack's son didn't seem interested.

Jack was furious that Emilio had spoken with a competitor, but didn't say anything. Jack's lawyer said to be very careful because he had seen this situation before. Once an employee starts to get unrealistic dreams of owning a company they can quickly become a liability. The lawyer agreed with Jack that a sales rep would not have the technical skills to run the company.

The lawyer told Jack about "golden handcuff" agreements: the employee gets shares but will lose those shares if they leave the company. The employee has to have "skin in the game," meaning real money to buy the shares. Jack liked the idea of the golden handcuffs. Jack agreed that if Emilio had skin in the game he would be less likely to cause trouble.

The accountant told the business valuator who was determining the share price to make the assumption that the customer base was diversified and that there was good management in place. MarMac was valued at $6 million. The plan was to sell 5% of the shares to Emilio for $300,000. Emilio did his best to work through and understand the 48-page shareholder's agreement. Finally he told Jack that he and his wife were concerned that paying half the money up front would take them past the borrowing limit on their home. Jack's lawyer said he saw this coming; Emilio was not sufficiently committed.

Six months later Emilio quit and went to work for QuantaTool. Almost immediately Emilio's customers stopped sending work to MarMac and sales went down almost 20%.

Jack's lawyer sought a court order to stop Emilio from working at QuantaTool. Emilio defended on the basis that the non-competition clause in the MarMac employment agreement was unreasonable. After a year of back and forth and $100,000 in legal fees, Jack's lawyer recommended dropping the lawsuit, saying, "At least we slowed him down."

During the second half of 2007 and into 2008 Jack's larger customers started taking longer to pay, from 60 days to 120 days. This stretched MarMac's own ability to pay. Jack went to the bank to get an extension on his line of credit to $1.5 million. The bank valued MarMac at $6.5 million. The bank also asked for a personal guarantee and a mortgage on Jack's home, where he had lived with his wife for more than 30 years. His home was worth $400,000, it was fully paid off and it was the only asset Jack had outside of his business.

Jack was 70 years old by this time and had been operating his business for almost 35 years; he had seen bad times before. His accountant told him that it was fairly standard for the bank to ask for a personal guarantee. The chance of the bank going after a $400,000 home when the business was worth $6.5 million seemed quite small.

In 2009 Jack's largest customer, Navistar, closed its plant and overnight Jack lost 60% of his business and $1 million in receivables. Within months the bank demanded payment on the line of credit. Word went out, MarMac's best employees left and long-term customers wouldn't return calls.

The seriousness of the situation really sunk in the day Jack and his wife were evicted from their home. During Jack's bankruptcy hearing the bank's lawyer was very aggressive about where all the money had gone. The bank received only $1.5 million on the liquidation. Where did the other $5 million go?

Jack sat through it all without much to say; he himself didn't really understand how $5 million could evaporate so quickly. What he didn't know was that the valuation was for the purposes of maximizing his financing; it had not been conducted to identify the areas of his business that needed improvement. But Jack had not committed fraud and there was no dishonest dealing; the business had just disappeared. The bank had nothing to go on, so Jack received his discharge from bankruptcy shortly after his 73rd birthday. The only income he had was what he and his wife received as a minimal government pension.

Succession in the Court of Appeal

Sometimes business owners do have a plan but fear that the succession process will cause conflict in the family, so they don't formalize their plan and they don't communicate it. But that communication failure can devastate families. Let me tell you another story, about another man named Jack, this one taken from the decision written by the Ontario Court of Appeal. It's a story about several failures: failure to plan, failure to collaborate and failure of the litigation system.

The court decision is called *Mountain v. TD Canada Trust*. The case centered on the Mountain family farm, which had been in the family for five generations, since 1830. Jack Mountain, the owner, may not have had faith in the court system. But by failing to complete his succession planning, he left litigation as the only option to resolve the legacy of dispute he left his son and daughter.

Gary Mountain, Jack's son, had been working on the farm for 24 years, since high school. In the beginning he received less-than-average wages so that money could be put back into the farm to build it up. Over time father and son came to act as partners on the farm and on many occasions Jack promised Gary the farm would pass to him. Gary's sister, Louanne, had never worked on the farm.

A common issue in family farms, and other family businesses, is dealing with the non-active children like Louanne, who do not work in the business. How do you treat active and non-active children fairly? It is not uncommon for a farm to be worth $10 million. If you plan to give the farm to the farming child, what do you give non-farming children? History has shown that it is very difficult for on-farm and off-farm children to cooperate in the ownership of a farm (or any business).

A common misconception is that the on-farm child is getting $10 million if their parents leave the farm to them. But a farm is not money in the bank. If the farm is to stay in the family, the on-farm child is just getting a job, plus a responsibility to manage the family legacy.

Decades earlier, Jack and his wife, Helen, had written identical wills – the type that every storefront law office sells for $99. They all follow the same pattern:

1. When the first spouse dies all of his or her estate goes to the second spouse.

2. When the second spouse dies, whatever is left is divided equally among the children.

This pattern of equal property division makes sense in most cases. But with a family farm or a family business this approach to property division can create havoc. In the Mountain case, based on the wording of the old will, one-half of the farm was transferred to Louanne after her parents died. Gary launched a lawsuit to enforce the oral agreement he had with his father that the farm was to go to him.

Before he died, Jack had made a number of attempts to transfer the farm to Gary. A year before his death Jack met with Mr. Riley, his book-keeper. Riley explained that Jack could transfer the farm property to Gary tax-free. Riley made detailed notes of the discussion with Jack confirming that Jack wanted to transfer the farm to Gary.

In October 2001 Jack was diagnosed with terminal cancer and hospitalized. A lawyer friend recommended that Jack sign powers of attorney. A power of attorney allows someone else to sign checks and legal and banking documents on your behalf.

While still in hospital Jack signed a power of attorney, prepared by a second lawyer who visited Jack at hospital, giving Gary full control over the farm and its bank accounts. Despite the fact that Jack had recently been diagnosed with terminal cancer, it was confirmed at the trial that this lawyer did not ask Jack about his will or any land transfers.

After being released from the hospital in early November Jack met with Mr. Riley again. Riley sent a letter to Jack, dated November 13, 2001, once again confirming that Jack wanted to transfer the farm to Gary and that Louanne would get a small house, life insurance and an investment account.

Jack made an appointment with a third lawyer for November 15. Unfortunately Jack never got to see this lawyer: he was readmitted to hospital before that and died on November 28.

Gary did not have any luck in court. After an 11-day trial the judge decided that Jack did not intend to transfer the property to his son. The only document in writing was the decades-old will. The judge said, "Jack had thoughts about how to arrange his affairs, knew that they had not been put in place and did not put them in place."

There was no dispute that Jack had promised for years to transfer the farm to Gary. If Jack did not intend to transfer the farm, did this mean he had been lying to Gary all that time? No one seems to have asked that question.

The judge dismissed Gary's case and ordered him to pay $275,000 in legal costs to Louanne. Gary appealed the decision to the Ontario Court of Appeal. This time he had better luck – he won. The appeal court thought it was more likely that the swift deterioration in Jack's health prevented him from completing the farm transfer and referred to the following evidence:

> » Several witnesses, including Louanne, testified that while Jack was in the hospital, he indicated he wanted to meet with a lawyer.
> » The third lawyer testified that he was expecting there to be a transfer of the farm property to Gary.
> » A minister testified that on November 18 or 19, 2001, Jack told him that he had just "told Gary to take the farm and get a lawyer to have it settled."

Because of the complexity of issues the appeal court judges ordered a new trial and set aside the $275,000 in costs that Gary had to pay Louanne. They also ordered Louanne to pay Gary $40,000 in costs. In spite of ordering a new trial the appeal court judge who wrote the decision said, "I must stress that a new trial is in neither side's interest. This case cries out for a mediated, consensual resolution."

What did Gary and Louanne get after spending more than half a million dollars in legal fees and months of effort preparing for trial? The answer is a lot of grief. This case clearly portrays a failure in communication and collaboration that commonly plagues families in business and their advisors. In hindsight it seems obvious that at least one of the lawyers should have called Mr. Riley, the bookkeeper.

So what's the solution? How do you make sure your story doesn't become a cautionary tale? Read on.

The Emergency Exit

Before diving into a discussion about value creation, we need to pause and reflect on where we are. Business succession planning is brought on by the fact that we are all getting older. Increased health, technology and lifespan allow business owners to stay in their companies longer, making it easier to postpone business succession planning. But you should be planning now for life into your nineties; the reality is that there is a whole *new third stage of life* that just didn't exist when we were born. You really should be thinking now about what your life will be like in your nineties.

That thinking should include how you are going to give up control of your business, because no one can control a business forever. At some point the owner and the business will part ways. This parting can be delayed until the death of the owner but in most cases it happens sooner. The question is whether the parting is planned or an emergency.

· · · · · · · · · · · · · · · ·

Succession planning is too often done only
as a result of an emergency.

· · · · · · · · · · · · · · · ·

According to the Exit Planning Institute in Chicago the emergency exits are often described as the "Six Ds": death, disablement, debt, dispute, disaster and divorce. They say that 55% of all business exits occur as a result of one of those six emergencies. International business advisory firm Grant Thornton agrees. Jack Martin exited MarMac through debt; Jack Mountain left his farm through death.

An emergency exit is useful in a fire, but when a business owner is taken to emergency it is the business that is on fire. All too often family members are left to sift through the ashes. The purpose of planning is to be able to walk out the front door.

Inadequate Succession Planning

How big is the problem? To help them decide which industries they will lend money to, banks examine economic trends; one of those trends relates to business succession. In November 2012 the Canadian Imperial Bank of Commerce (CIBC) released a report called *Inadequate Business Succession Planning—A Growing Macroeconomic Risk*.

Macroeconomic means affecting the entire economy. Normally we think of inadequate succession planning as a risk to individual business owners. CIBC's report examines the macroeconomic risks – that is, the effect on the Canadian economy as a whole – of the inadequate business succession planning that has been repeatedly demonstrated by surveys. The bank found the following:

> Close to 30%, or 310,000, of business owners will exit ownership or transfer control of their businesses within five years. Within the next ten years, one-half (or 550,000) of owners will exit their business… In the coming five years, an estimated $1.9 trillion in business assets are poised to change hands – the largest turnover of economic control on record. And by 2022, this number will mushroom to no less than $3.7 trillion.

In its report CIBC notes that this lack of succession planning is understandable – small business owners don't have the resources to do it and they're struggling to stay profitable. There may be disagreement among co-owners about the future of the business and they may not communicate or deal with conflict well. CIBC agreed with other researchers that succession planning is too often done only as a result of an emergency in the business.

The only part that I and most exit planners disagree with CIBC on is the timeframe. The bank is probably using historical retirement data but it seems that most business owners now expect to work longer than owners used to. However, a delay will not avoid the actuaries; the 55% of owners who fail to plan will still be using the emergency exit.

The Human Capital of the Owner

The CIBC report also commented on the human capital of the owner: "At this stage of the game, a small business's principal strength – the reliance on the human capital of the owner in almost every aspect of the business – is also becoming its primary weakness."

This statement captures the essence of the problem.

Capital is the amount of money, or value, employed in a business – the amount someone would pay for the business. Human capital is not money, it's the stock of competencies, knowledge and social and personality attributes, including creativity, cognitive abilities and experience, of the humans in the business.

Reliance on the human capital of the owner means the owner is holding the business together. If the owner left, the business would collapse. Without the owner there would be no business. This does not mean there is no value in the business, it just means there is no value without the owner. This fact explains why many business owners are confused when they are told that their business, which may generate $500,000 a year in profit, will be worth only $1 million if they sell it. The problem is that the value cannot be transferred. This type of non-transferable value is called personal goodwill.

A business has tangible and intangible assets. Tangible assets can be seen and touched: property, equipment and inventory. When a business is liquidated it is sold for the value of its tangible assets. The liquidation value is the lowest value for which a business can be sold – and it's often the value realized for a lifestyle business.

Intangible assets are assets we cannot touch. Some intangible assets, such as the business name and logo, can be seen but other important assets, such as goodwill, cannot. Goodwill refers to the affection the market has for the business, measured in terms of the amount and quality of business the company can attract.

· · · · · · · · · · · · · · · ·

A small business's principal strength – the reliance on the human capital of the owner – is also becoming its primary weakness.

· · · · · · · · · · · · · · · ·

Goodwill is often a company's most significant value. The world's most valuable brand in 2014 is Apple, followed by Microsoft and then… Google? No – it's number five. Sitting at number three is an old-fashioned soda company: Coca-Cola. Perhaps we're not surprised because the name Coca-Cola is so familiar – but we should be. How does Coca-Cola change the world or add value?

At the 2010 Innovation Forum, world-leading valuation expert Aswath Damodaran described the intrinsic value of Coca-Cola's product:

> Soda is water with a bunch of sugar and a lot of crap thrown in. You can put whatever you want on the outside of the can, but there is really no difference between one cola and another cola.

You may say that Coca-Cola tastes different – that's what 100 years of playing with your mind does to you... The cola business is all about branding, not the product.

Despite his obvious disdain Damodaran valued Coca-Cola's business at $80 billion. Of that amount only $16 billion is attributable to all the factories, equipment and offices that Coca-Cola owns. The rest, a whopping $64 billion, or 80% of the company's value, comes from goodwill alone.

Remember that goodwill is the attractive force that causes people to choose one product over another – and this is important – regardless of the intrinsic merits of the product. This attractive force can be measured in the amount that is charged for a product and in the additional sales that a product like Coke enjoys over a competitor such as RC Cola. You could say the value of a business is the value of the tangible assets plus the attractive force of those assets. Remove the attractive force and what you have left is a pile of stuff but not a lot of value.

Let's roll this back to a lifestyle business. It is the human capital of the owner that's the attractive force. Removing the owner is like switching off the current to an electromagnet – everything falls to the floor. That's why a business that can generate $500,000 per year in profit might be worth only $1 million or less in a sale. Coca-Cola can sell its goodwill but the attractive force of the owner cannot be sold. It is *personal* goodwill that walks out the door with the owner. In Chapter 3 I refer to this as value quicksand and it's the owner who is sinking.

Risk – The Value Buster

Personal goodwill is bad enough – but it gets worse. Risk has a huge impact on the value of a lifestyle business. The more involved the owner is the higher the risk. It is a simple formula, really. Remember the Six Ds we discussed earlier? There is a statistical probability that one of those six will happen to any of us. It may not, but it *could*, and an actuary can figure out with a high degree of certainty how many people in a million will fall victim.

Risk makes business valuators crazy. And there are dozens of different types of risks. Even things that "cannot happen" – black swan events –

happen regularly. So when an investor calls a valuator to review the purchase of a small business and asks, "What is the likelihood I will earn a return on my investment?" the valuator responds, "Very small."

RISK REDUCES VALUE

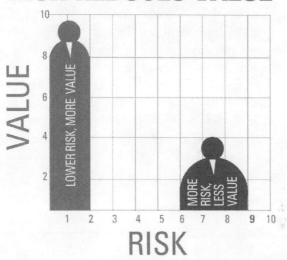

If you compare the value of a lifestyle business with the value of money in the bank, you will realize how risky valuators think lifestyle businesses are. Imagine a business that's worth $1 million. If the business owner becomes disabled the $1 million value of the business could evaporate quickly. But $1 million in the bank could stay and grow forever no matter what happens to the owner or the business.

"Hold on," you say, "the interest on my $1 million bank account is only $30,000 a year; I'd rather have the business and make $500,000 a year." True enough, but understand that the reason for the big difference in the return is the risk. A lifestyle business is great while you can operate it, but if you are disabled and you can't operate the business it has no value. At that point you would much rather have $1 million in the bank. If someone were to ask a valuator, "What is the value of a lifestyle business that generates $500,000 a year?" the valuator would reply, "Very little."

In the big picture there are two types of risk: systemic and non-systemic (or un-systemic).

Systemic risk is risk in the economy and society as a whole. Drought is a systemic risk because lack of water affects everyone through rising prices and food shortages. A stock market crash is a systemic risk because it affects everyone who participates in the economy. Rising interest rates are a systemic risk. Valuators see the entire economy as a seething cauldron of systemic risks.

Non-systemic risk does not affect the entire economic system. It affects only an individual. Non-systemic risk arises because of the personal characteristics and behaviors of the lifestyle business owner. The most common non-systemic risks are lack of delegation and lack of documentation of lifestyle business processes. If the lifestyle business owner can't show up for work for the next three months, there is no one to ask and no manuals to refer to. How is the business supposed to carry on?

Bringing it all together, inadequate business succession planning is a non-systemic risk that affects so many lifestyle business owners that it has become a systemic risk.

Boomer Bust

Boomer business owners face additional problems caused by the demographics of the Baby Boom itself. In his book *Beating the Boomer Bust,* US author John F. Dini points out that 20 to 30 years after the Baby Boom there was a business start-up boom. Boomers were growing up and opening record numbers of businesses. After the mid-1960s birth rates declined substantially to levels even lower than they had been before the boom. Dini's concern is that the excess number of Boomer businesses cannot be absorbed by the younger generation.

Dini calculates that in the US there are six million Boomer businesses. This translates into 1,000 businesses being transferred, undergoing succession or disappearing in the US every day for the next 20 years. This six million is a little more than 10 times the 550,000 Canadian Boomer businesses – 100 per day for the next 20 years – that CIBC predicts will be transferred or disappear.

Business succession itself is not news – it's been around since the first business and it has applied to every business since. The news in Canada is the value ($3.8 trillion) and the number of transactions (hundreds of thousands). This is not some faraway war or the sound of phantom derivative dollars imploding as the stock market crashes; it's real.

The challenge is this: will there be wealth preservation or will there be widespread destruction of value in family businesses across the continent? CIBC is concerned that the destruction will be so great that the economy itself will suffer.

Is the Lifestyle Business Responsible for the Business Succession Crisis?

In a lifestyle business, the lifestyle of the owner is more important than maximizing the value of the business. Lifestyle businesses often grow to the size of the inside of the owner's head; once the demands of the business exceed the owner's available time the business stops growing. As long as the owner can continue to return phone calls the business grows; when the owner reaches his or her phone call limit the business stops growing.

Observers often point to lifestyle businesses as the source of the business succession crisis. They say that lifestyle businesses are never ready for sale. By contrast, a professionally run business is always near sale-ready. This is not a function of wanting to be sale-ready; it is simply the natural consequence of ensuring that there are proper systems in place, accountability, incentives, delegation, reporting and a clear growth strategy. Lifestyle entrepreneurs view these topics as bureaucratic fussiness; what's worse is that they're right. It is impossible to be any more efficient, or to reduce administrative expense any further, than running the entire business out of the inside of your head.

A true lifestyle business grows organically around the present needs of the owner and their family, slowly evolving over time to generate the income, schedule and community best suited to the family lifestyle. Friendly underperforming employees stay and best practices are ignored: "why would we do that?" The hallmarks of the lifestyle entrepreneur are blissful ignorance and the unquestioned assumption that life and business will never change. And for decades that can be true. But the locomotive of time and change stops for no one.

Another problem is the enormousness of the succession undertaking. It is impossible to accomplish all the transactions that need to be undertaken to become sale-ready in one engagement with one advisor. Given the number of skill sets required – corporate, estate, tax, human resources, valuation and accounting – it is nearly impossible for a small firm to handle the entire job. There is clearly a need for a process that brings all these disciplines together.

In larger cases, mergers and acquisitions (M&A) specialists handle business transactions. But these larger cases represent only a tiny fraction of the number of businesses in the succession market. The M&A market will look only at certain sizes of transactions. In the first tier, only companies with a value of $100 million or more will be considered; in the second tier only companies with a value of $5 million to $100 million are considered.

Companies valued at less than $5 million are not considered large enough to merit the attention of an M&A firm. This smaller market is served by business brokers, many of whom are quite competent, but I know of only a handful of experienced brokers. The under–$5 million market has hundreds of thousands of businesses. It represents a large opportunity.

Despite the lack of attention the M&A community pays to small businesses, practices developed by the M&A and large-business community can benefit smaller businesses. Don't forget that all big businesses, unless they were spin-offs, emerged from the small business market. Many of the practices that make larger companies more valuable apply in the small business market. After all, what's the difference between a big business and a small one? Two zeroes. What do two zeroes do for our $1 million business? It becomes a $100 million business.

All of the concepts discussed in this book are worth two zeroes: value creation, team building and employee share ownership have undergone decades of development and follow fairly well-defined paths. These ideas work for an eight-zero business and they will work for a six-zero or five-zero business. You don't have to be Amazon.com to become a great company.

But ironically it is *lifestyle* that is the clear focus of the best succession plans. This means we are not trying to change the business into a professionally run, high-growth M&A target. What we are trying to do is create enough new value that the business can finance the owner's lifestyle requirements during the third stage of life and also leave enough money on the table so that the successor is motivated to stay around. If the successor wants to keep going – to eight, nine or 10 zeroes – that's fine, but it's not really the focus of this book.

In the next chapter we consider what *exiting* feels like and we test whether or not you can sell your business. If you can sell right now for the price you need, you don't need to go through the effort involved in hiring your buyer.

Chapter 2

Can I Sell My Business? The Value Gap

The Dark Side of Exiting

TRYING TO MAKE A DECISION about business succession can be painful and riddled with emotional confusion or it can just leave you numb – there's no feeling, just passive resistance. The decision never gets made.

Part of the reason is that the idea of slowing down and even quitting goes against the grain of the entrepreneurial spirit. If you do an Internet search for "entrepreneurial traits" you will find numerous lists, most of which seem to work against the idea of business succession planning:

> » Many entrepreneurs live by the motto "when you do what you love you never have to work a day in your life."
> » You cannot expect to be effective and successful in business unless you truly believe in your business and in the goods and services you sell.

It's no surprise you wouldn't want to give up what you love or something you believe in. In addition to the feeling that exiting goes against the entrepreneurial grain, many well-established relationships will change or even end when you leave your business. Once we start tromping around your business and pulling the weeds, your life will get very murky for a while.

Harry's life got murky when he sold his small business. He received a good price and had enough money to enjoy retirement, but he couldn't.

Harry was a sad, aging man who reflected constantly on the emptiness of his life. He had never spent time developing interests outside of his business. And the prospect of spending time with a spouse who really didn't want him hanging around the house all day made him all the more depressed.

For people like Harry the public recognition that comes with owning a successful business becomes the most meaningful dimension of their lives. They have power over employees, they wine and dine customers and get wined and dined by suppliers. They go to expensive offices to see professionals and discuss important confidential matters. They show up at charity functions with checks and sit on boards. In short, their business roots them deeply into the community.

When they sell the business or make plans for succession they're uprooted like a tree blown over in a storm. The feeling of falling is often made worse by the fact that normal roots – a fulfilling personal life; good relationships with a spouse, children and friends; and outside contacts and interests – are absent. That's one reason many business owners delay retiring and cling to power as long as they can.

I once saw a cartoon showing a small 95-year-old man with his arm around his taller 70-year-old son. They are looking at a sprawling complex of factories, smokestacks and warehouses. The caption reads, "Someday, son, this will all be yours."

Sometimes the way owners behaved while they were running the business affects their decision about exit and succession. The Japanese movie *Ran* is about the once-invincible, now aging, warlord Hidetora, patriarch of the Ichimonji clan. Hidetora has reached the top through the most ruthless of methods. Along the way he brutally exterminated many important families, hunting down survivors and eliminating children who may seek revenge. The fear of a slow and painful death was his most eloquent management technique.

Now in his 70s, Hidetora decides to divide his kingdom among his three sons: Taro, Jiro and Saburo. Hidetora illustrates his plan by showing that one arrow can easily be broken, but not three arrows together. However, his most loyal son, Saburo, knows his brother Jiro is disloyal, so he smashes the three arrows across his knee and calls the lesson stupid. Hidetora mistakes disagreement for a threat and banishes Saburo from the kingdom.

The balance of the movie chronicles one emotionally unintelligent decision after another, all based on lack of communication, as each member of Hidetora's extended family is slowly exterminated. Hidetora goes into hiding and slowly descends into madness. At the end Saburo finally finds his father, filthy and almost unrecognizable, wandering in the wilderness. The two are reunited and Hidetora comes briefly to his senses. However, Saburo is shot and killed by snipers sent out by his brother Jiro. Overcome with grief, Hidetora dies. Jiro dies in battle soon after, marking the end of the Ichimonji clan.

The movie is a dramatic example but I know of an owner of a construction business who used a constant stream of litigation to intimidate and bankrupt many smaller competitors and suppliers. At 84 he still went to the office every day, even on Sunday mornings. He was trapped. He had no skills that would allow him to venture outside his office or off a jobsite. This doesn't mean you shouldn't go to work at 84, it simply means you should have other choices.

Most business owners are woefully negligent in their understanding of the psychological dynamics of succession. The default mode is simply to abandon succession rather than find help to prepare for such a critical life change.

The case of Stephanie, who owned a high-end solar window company, illustrates a successful transition. In this succession plan, the oldest member of the employee-led buyout team was 24 years younger than Stephanie. Stephanie proposed and the team accepted a special work arrangement for the hard-to-replace experienced owner who no longer wanted to run the company full time but still wanted to be engaged in meaningful work.

With the support of the employee buyout group, Stephanie developed a plan for slowing down and shifting responsibility. She had always enjoyed the public relations aspect of the company – she had gotten the company quite involved in the support of a mission in Haiti that built schools. Through her impassioned support and commitment she had developed a wide network of owners and senior executives who often did business with her or referred others to her. The buyout team had great respect for Stephanie and appreciated both the importance of the work in Haiti and how that work benefited the company. Together with Stephanie, the buyout team worked out a flexible, phased retirement policy that allowed her to reduce the hours she worked and to work in a different capacity. This flexible approach allowed Stephanie to transition gradually, in contrast to the abrupt termination common when a company is sold.

In this instance, Stephanie became a special advisor to the buyout team and led the company's public relations efforts by attending social functions and traveling to Haiti three or four times a year. The arrangement not only helped the employee buyout group to adjust to running the company, it gave space for both Stephanie and her husband to experiment with non-workplace activities without having her leave the workplace altogether. What's more, Stephanie's husband had been the one who had founded the Haiti mission, making Stephanie's ongoing work something both could engage in.

Arrangements like Stephanie's are win-wins for both the buyout team and the transitioning owner. Given the damage that can be caused by a powerful owner's struggle to retain control and identity, managing a slow transition out of the business can be at least as important as managing the training and development of the buyout team coming in.

Should You Hire Your Buyer?

The answer is no – if you don't need to. If you know you can sell your business for the money you need, you need a broker, not this book.

The standard advice is to sell your business if you can. The main reason is that selling eliminates risk because you have the money instead. My advice is that you should not proceed with a hire your buyer plan unless you clearly understand why you are doing it. The main reason is that when you hire your buyer you introduce risk – the plan may not work. The second reason is that a hire your buyer plan requires a focused effort; you shouldn't start unless you have clear objectives in mind.

If you read this book and improve the value and salability of your business to the point where you can satisfy your objectives, then sell if that works. In other words, anytime you can take the off-ramp, you should. On the other hand, if you want a long tail on the phaseout from your business this book leads the way.

It is important to understand your motivations in business succession. Your motivations dictate your choices, which dictate your outcomes.

There are three basic scenarios:

- » Sell your business as soon as reasonably possible.
- » Develop a multiyear succession plan.
- » Stay involved as long as possible (ride it out).

The first choice you have to make is whether you want to sell your business as soon as reasonably possible. You may be bored, burned out or facing a health crisis. On the other hand, you may be in complete control and confident you can sell your business. You need to decide:

- » Sale – will my business sell?
- » Value – how will it be valued?
- » Value gap – will I have enough money to meet my lifestyle needs?

There are no reliable statistics on small business sales but it may be that only 10% of small businesses sell for an amount the owner is happy with. Owners have to ensure that once their business income is gone they have sufficient net worth and sources of income to support their lifestyle in the third stage of life. If not, there is a value gap.

Storage Wars:
How Most Buyers See Your Business

Unless it's on a toxic waste dump, almost every business has a liquidation value. To understand liquidation value think of the reality TV show *Storage Wars*, which is about a group of pawnshop owners who bid against each other to buy the contents of abandoned storage lockers.

The abandoned locker gets cut open and the prospective buyers look in and quickly try to determine a value based on what they can see from the outside. The fun part of the show is when the winner of the bid picks through the locker's contents. They open suitcases and boxes, adding up the value of what they find to see whether they made or lost money on the locker. Most of the time the stuff is junk but sometimes there are antiques, coins and valuable collectibles.

Most buyers look at your business the same way – as a locker full of junk. Maybe the business has some valuable assets tucked away that help turn a profit; maybe not. Many successful business owners go to equipment and machinery auctions expecting to pay 10 cents on the dollar. Unless your business has transferable goodwill or some strategic value, you won't get much.

Even when a business is not liquidated through an auction, it may not bring very much. BizBuySell.com is the largest US business sale listing website. It receives 10 million page views a month. The average value of the business sales it tracked in 2011 was $155,000. So when someone tells you your business will sell, you should reply, "Yes, I know it will sell, but how much will it sell for?" What you really need to know is whether your business will sell for the amount you need or want. If not, you have a value gap.

10 Factors That Increase Odds of an Offer

The Sellability Score, developed by John Warrillow, is one of the tools on the web that can help you assess the current transferability or "sellability" of your business. On the Sellability Score website you can take a short quiz for free and receive a report that gives you some interesting information. You will also get a follow-up email from a consultant.

In 2012, Sellability Score researchers analyzed results from users over the previous 12 months. The research team compared businesses that had received an offer to buy with those that had not received an offer. The sample included 2,300 companies from around the world; the majority were in Canada, the US, the UK, Australia and Ireland. It identified 10 factors that increase the odds of receiving an offer for your business. The following are the first three:

» The business can survive without you – you are nearly twice as likely to get an offer if your business can thrive without you.
» Your top sales person is replaceable – you are twice as likely to receive an offer if you could easily replace your most important sales or marketing person.
» You are not responsible for most sales – you are more than twice as likely to get an offer if you are personally responsible for less than 75% of sales.

The list goes on, identifying various aspects of the business that need to be replaceable – in other words, a business that depends on a person or relationship that cannot be replaced is very vulnerable. Another important factor is the size of the business. Sellability Score reports that a business with annual revenue of over $3 million is twice as likely to receive an offer as a business with less than $500,000 in revenue.

Importantly, and hearkening back to the idea of the human capital of the owner, Sellability Score reports that having a formal management team doubles your chances of receiving an offer.

The last point we will review from the Sellability list is recurring revenue. Recurring revenue arises when sales reliably repeat without additional marketing costs or effort. When Sears sells a vacuum the vacuum bags are recurring revenue; when a dealership sells a car the oil changes and repairs are recurring revenue. Imagining ways to create recurring revenue is useful because businesses with more than 25% recurring revenue will receive – you guessed it – double the number of offers as businesses without recurring revenue.

Business Valuation Basics

It is important to understand business valuation principles because sale prices are based on some form of business valuation. Some of the concepts in the rest of this section are technical and may be hard to follow but it's worth the effort. Speak with your accountant or a business valuator to ensure you understand the principles as they relate to your business.

FIRST 2 ELEMENTS OF VALUE

FREE CASH FLOW **X** MULTIPLE

The most common misconception about business value is that a business has only one value. But value has dozens of variations. Three common ones are liquidation value, book value and fair market value (FMV). Others are replacement value, insurance value and expropriation value. Shareholders are not immune – shares can be valued at control value, minority value or fair value.

FMV is often thought of as the value at which a business will sell; it is the theoretical price that a business will sell for on the open market for 100% cash on closing. But FMV is based on assumptions. Change the assumptions and you change the value. It is hypothetical, made up and only as good as the information and assumptions it is based on. Garbage in, garbage out.

In one case the tax authorities based the FMV of a gravel operation on four times (4×) cash flow. This FMV was based on the assumption that the quarry would produce the same amount of gravel forever. When it was pointed out that the gravel would run out in less than 10 years and that this would be followed by environmental cleanup costs, the value dropped by 80%. Anytime you review a valuation you have to *understand the assumptions* it is based on.

A really good test of a valuation is whether it feels right. Never, ever assume a professional knows more about your business than you do. If the value seems wrong or doesn't make sense seek another opinion, and keep going until it does feel right. Make sure you understand the assumptions it is based on. Ask the valuator to explain why those assumptions were used and others ignored. The valuator opens a new file tomorrow but you only get one shot. You may be wrong but you should always dig until you are sure.

The reason for a second opinion is that FMV is simply one valuator's theory. Many court cases have dealt with valuation issues. Rarely do two valuation experts agree on FMV and often their conclusions are far apart. This is so common that many judges look at two valuations as a range of possible values. One valuation is at the high end of the range and the second valuation is at the low end. Often a judge will simply pick a value in the middle. Does anyone believe this is the *real* value? No. It is just a value that can be used as a justification in a court decision.

No matter how good the valuation is, unless a real buyer exists who agrees with it, you will never get that price. Consider the television show *Shark Tank*. The entrepreneurs seeking investors have to put a valuation on their companies. There always seems to be one investor who never agrees with anyone's valuation. The investor will say the entrepreneur is asking five times what the company is worth or that they are crazy – or both. Either way, the entrepreneur gets kicked out.

The Three Approaches in a Business Valuation Report

Out of the dozens of approaches to value, a business valuation report will usually discuss three: liquidation value, comparative value and going concern value.

I've already discussed liquidation value, the locker full of junk approach.

Comparative value is the way your house is valued by your real estate agent. Comparative value for houses is easy because there are thousands of houses for sale at publicly disclosed prices. The comparative approach is difficult with small businesses because many small businesses are unique. The more unique your business is, the less likely there will be comparable businesses to refer to.

There are developing sources of information for comparative values: BizBuySell.com claims to have enough data on certain types of businesses – pizzerias, flower shops, etc. – to do comparisons. For certain types of businesses you can get a realistic comparative value from BizBuySell for less than $200. Another website, BizEquity.com, claims to be the world's largest provider of business valuations. As of May 2014 it has "valued over 13,145,006 companies and counting." BizEquity charges less than $400 for a valuation.

Going concern value is based on the assumption that the business is going to continue in operation. This means that it is worth more operating than it is liquidated. To determine going concern value, ask what the cash flow is each year and what that cash flow is worth. In other words, the buyer says, "I am paying you money for your business. What is the return on my investment (ROI)?" The answer to this question is tied up in the two iconic business valuation concepts: *free cash flow* and *a multiple*.

. . . .

To determine going concern value, ask what the cash flow is each year and what that cash flow is worth.

. . . .

Free cash flow (also referred to as "earning power") is not the same as profit. Most people assume that profit is the return on investment. But profit is not a reliable number for investment purposes. When we calculate profit we need to make a number of accounting adjustments. For instance, the business may have lost money several years ago, but because we have profit this year we use those losses to reduce the profit and pay less tax. Reducing profit by using old losses actually increases free cash flow because we pay less tax.

The next important step is determining the value of that free cash flow. Business valuators will often use the *discounted cash flow* (DCF) method. The DCF method involves a determination of what the free cash flow will be in the future and how much an investor should pay today to buy that future stream of free cash flow. Because that free cash flow is not guaranteed in the future, that cash flow is discounted because of a multitude of systemic and non-systemic risks. In addition the net present value – the value of those future dollars today – is calculated.

For our purposes it is sufficient to work with a multiple rather than going through the calculations required by the DCF method. A multiple is perfectly useful for illustration purposes because we are developing a keen sense of the factors that affect value so we can work with them. The reason I raise DCF in the first place is to point out that there are many other more sophisticated methods that you can and should discuss with your accountant and/or valuator if you are contemplating a real valuation.

A Multiple of Free Cash Flow

A simple way to estimate business value is to determine a *multiple* of *free cash flow*. In this method the buyer multiplies free cash flow to determine a price to pay for the business. Let's say free cash flow is $400,000 annually. If the business is controlled by the owner the buyer will consider the business quite risky and may be prepared to pay only a 2.5× multiple of cash flow (2.5 × $400,000 = $1 million). In valuation terms this is known as a *key man* or *key person discount*.

Here is the interesting part: let's say you delegate responsibility in your business and put proper processes in place, which lowers the risk. Now the buyer may agree to a higher multiple – say a 5× multiple. This may mean the buyer is prepared to pay $2 million (5 × $400,000). This represents a $1 million difference in valuation for the same business. The only real difference is the level of risk. By delegating and putting processes in place we have reduced the risks if something happens to the owner. Change the risks and you change the value. This is why risk is such an important issue in valuation.

Determining Your Business's Value

The simple formula "free cash flow × multiple" has dozens of variations depending on the valuator and the situation, but they all circle around some measure of cash flow that is multiplied (or discounted) in some way.

. . . .

Here is the interesting part: let's say you delegate responsibility in your business and put proper processes in place, which lowers the risk. Now the buyer may agree to a higher multiple.

. . . .

In the Appendix to this book, "Seven Steps for Determining Business Value," I've provided a step-by-step formula that will give you a basic indication of what the buyer's advisors may be telling the buyer about the value of your business. This value will probably be the starting point unless you are dealing with a strategic buyer. The concept of strategic buyer is discussed below.

If you want to look at the sale process in more depth, you can contact a chartered business valuator or look at BizBuySell.com, which provides an extensive free resource of over 100 pages that contains a dozen questionnaires designed to guide you through the business sale decision-making process.

Value Gap

A value gap occurs when you do not have enough assets to support your lifestyle in the third stage of life. What you need to know is this: what will it cost to retire, and do you have enough? This includes lifestyle and legacy costs. There are a number of free online retirement income calculators you can use to get an idea of how much money you will need to finance your lifestyle to your life expectancy. You can also meet with a financial planner to work this out.

Once you know the cost of retirement and legacy, you need to understand your ability to fund this cost. The basic formula is your net worth plus the realizable value from your business. This realizable value includes income for the time you will continue to work and the amount you can realize if you sell. If you don't have enough, you have a value gap.

If you have a value gap, there are four alternatives: reduce the amount you spend in retirement, increase the return you get on your investments, work longer or create value in your business.

HOW TO CALCULATE THE VALUE GAP

The double-barreled advantage of the hire your buyer solution is that you can increase both the *amount of time* that you can draw income from your business while you slow down and the *amount of value* you can realize from your business as you transfer the equity.

Your Value Opportunity

An immediate step you can take that will increase the value of your business is to determine your "value opportunity." A company in Boston called Corporate Value Metrics has developed a sophisticated software product called the Value Opportunity Profile (VOP). There are a number of other software providers in this space, including CoreValue Software. VOP is the one I am most familiar with.

On its website, the designers of the VOP say,

Most private business owners never come close to maximizing the value of their businesses, purely because they aren't aware of the many factors that drive business value in the eyes of potential investors or acquirers.

Recently, several renowned experts conducted research that examined the differences in business values between public and private companies. They found that, on average, *a public company with no debt might be worth five times the value of a "comparable" private company.*

The VOP performs two functions: first, it analyzes your financial performance. Second, it asks 400 in-depth questions in eight categories.

These questions are designed to scrub each aspect of a business that M&A professionals consider during due diligence. Going through this process yourself in advance of due diligence puts you in the driver's seat.

The VOP gives you two pieces of valuable information: a value for your business that is often within 10% of the result of a full-blown valuation, and your score out of 10 in each of the eight categories (10 being what is expected in a world-class company). Most lifestyle businesses would score between three and six in each category (although the VOP designers don't say this, it makes sense that the multiple would follow along a similar point score). The lower you score, the lower the value and the greater your value opportunity – your value opportunity being the amount of value you can add to your business by correcting the deficiencies identified by the VOP software.

What makes the VOP software very cool is that you can see your value opportunity. Your value opportunity is what your company could be worth if its score was a perfect 10. The software designers recognize that most businesses will not get to 10, nor will they work on all eight categories. So there are buttons that will show what your value will be if you score eight across the board or 10 in one category and six in everything else. It lets you look at the categories you want to work on and see the effect of raising those scores by what you think you can accomplish. This way, you get instant feedback on the amount your value will increase if you improve those areas.

Strategic Value: A Locker Full of Good Stuff

Earlier in this chapter we discussed how a lot of buyers see your business as a locker full of junk, *Storage Wars*–style. There is another kind of buyer called a strategic buyer (or synergistic buyer). This buyer looks into the locker and sees a lot of good stuff. It's as if they see power tools, a dining room set and a new laptop – all things they need at home. Naturally this buyer will pay more – much more than a buyer who doesn't need any of it.

A strategic buyer will pay more than fair market value for your business because they are able to get more value out of it by combining your business with theirs. Maybe you have a customer list, a proprietary product, a technology – good stuff they can use to enhance their own business value. Perhaps you are a competitor they are eliminating.

Often, synergies are created by cost reductions, such as reducing office staff or combining factories. Instead of paying a 2 to 3× multiple, a synergistic buyer may be prepared to pay a 7× or even a 10× multiple. It is useful to speak with a broker or M&A professional to explore this possibility. You can also poke around your constellation of contacts to see if you can identify a strategic buyer. But waiting endlessly for a strategic buyer without planning will not end well.

10 Key Concerns When You Sell Your Business

Determining what your business could sell for is the first step in getting ready to sell it. Now you have to run the gauntlet of actually selling the business. There are 10 key concerns that may knock the value out of the deal:

1.   **The buyer has to choose you.** You have no control over the buyer. The buyer has to want your business and you have to convince the buyer and their advisory team that they should buy your business for a reasonable price on reasonable terms.

2.   **Due diligence is extensive.** The buyer does not know you or your business. The due diligence process is supposed to be confidential so the buyer has limited opportunity to interview inside employees. The only way the buyer can "know" your business is to know the documents that describe it. The production and review of paper is therefore extensive.

    Buyers have to rely on an extensive legal and accounting audit to get a true picture of the business. Many sellers are shocked by the amount of work it takes to satisfy due diligence requirements. That is why it is recommended that sellers conduct their own internal due diligence process up to two years in advance so they can be ready. This internal process also provides an opportunity to enhance business value.

3.   **You can set the price, if I can set the terms.** Owners think about price and buyers think about terms. The price has value only if the terms ensure that it will be paid, on time and in full.

Many buyers will agree to the owner's price "subject to due diligence" and grind the price down later. Some articles have stated that on average 15% gets knocked off the agreed price.

An extremely common request is vendor financing. That is, you do not get all your money on closing. In many cases the business has to meet growth and profit targets before you get paid. There is no guarantee that the vendor financing amount will be paid. A number of M&A articles have advised that you should not sign a deal unless the amount you get paid on closing is enough to satisfy your needs. That way, if the vendor financing amount is not paid you are not in trouble.

There are numerous other terms, such as working capital requirements and earn-outs, that require expert advice.

4. **Negotiation is an adversarial process.** An offer to sell a business will be reviewed by the purchaser's lawyer. Lawyers are hired to ensure that clients do not get ripped off; after all, it's the lawyer who is liable if something is overlooked. Lawyers can be quite obstinate in their negotiating positions. Knowing when to give in and when to walk away is important.

5. **The sale may fail.** There is a risk of sale failure before the sale. The buyer may get cold feet, the buyer may really only want information, an unexpected event may arise – a death, a stock market crash. Some M&A professionals estimate that only 20% of their engagements actually close successfully.

    Even when a deal does close there is still a 50–70% risk of after-sale failure. This risk is another reason to ensure you are happy with the amount you receive on closing.

6. **The buyer may only want your assets.** There are two ways to sell a business: sell shares or sell assets. In both Canada and the US the tax rate on capital gains is lower than the tax rate on asset sales. Canada has an additional advantage in that each shareholder can claim a personal capital gains exemption of $800,000 on the sale of qualifying small business shares.

What is good for the seller is not so good for the buyer. Buying shares has two disadvantages for the buyer: liabilities and depreciation.

» *Liabilities.* When a buyer buys shares they are buying the whole corporation and all of its history. There could be outstanding claims and lawsuits waiting in the wings. In fact this could be the reason the deal is so good. One company bought a 200-acre scrap yard for $1 million, only to discover that the new directors were personally liable for more than $9 million in environmental cleanup costs. The advantage of buying assets is that you can buy them without dragging historical liabilities along.

» *Depreciation.* When you buy assets you can take depreciation allowances. When you buy shares it is likely that the depreciation allowance has already been used and that there will be recapture liability.

7. **Price is based on FMV at closing.** Generally, the price paid for a business is based on FMV. The price for a private company is heavily discounted because of the risks of private company ownership. Arguably, FMV is the lowest price an owner can realize. There is also the risk that some or all of this price could be clawed back because of warranty or indemnity provisions.

8. **Control transfers to the buyer on closing.** Once you close the deal, the buyer owns and is now in control of the business. If you have not done sufficient due diligence on the buyer you may end up with someone who is dishonest and unethical and who may manipulate events to generate claims against you.

9. **You may have to pay commissions, sale expenses and taxes.** Always have your accountant calculate your net proceeds of the sale after expenses and taxes. Commissions may be 10% and other transaction costs and taxes may be as much as 50% of what's left. Make sure you are not surprised.

10. **Your work or consulting for the buyer will be defined, requiring reporting and targets.** Many owners describe the period during which they have to work for the new owners as "the two years of hell." Ron Joyce, who sold Tim Hortons to Wendy's, described the years after the sale as the worst of his business life. The Wendy's board made many mistakes and over 10 years the shares Joyce received from Wendy's lost hundreds of millions in value, not to mention the billions he would have made if he had kept his Tim Hortons shares instead.

Valuing and selling a business is not an easy process. Before you can even consider it you have to know whether you will get what you need from the sale. If you can get what you need then proceed with a sale. If you can't, the rest of this book sets out an approach that may help you. This approach requires that you be the kind of person who likes people and likes to see them succeed. If you are, and if you like building teams, read on. This approach may be for you.

In the next chapter we look at a systemic problem that small business owners find themselves in. The problem with the system created by the "I'm great, you're not" attitude we're about to discuss is that it makes it very difficult to hire your buyer and successfully build a value creation culture. Most small business professionals are so "great" they see no value in working with someone as "unimportant" as an employee.

Chapter 3

Value Quicksand:
I'm Great, You're Not

QUICKSAND FORMS when water seeps into one end of an enclosed sandy area and slowly seeps out the other side. The sand is suspended in the water and the surface appears solid. Most lifestyle businesses are built on value quicksand. The surface looks solid but when you reach down to try to pull the value out you find it's trapped. Remember Jack Martin? That's what happened to him.

The First Three Stages

There are many Jack Martins walking on quicksand. They work in lifestyle businesses without appreciating the risks involved, surrounded by professional advisors who do not appreciate the risks involved.

As a lawyer and business owner I tried for a long time to put my finger on the problems I saw in the small business community and among the professional advisors who served it. I finally stumbled across a great book by Dave Logan, John King and Halee Fischer-Wright called *Tribal Leadership: Leveraging Natural Groups to Build a Thriving Organization*.

The simple idea of *Tribal Leadership* is that human development as it relates to employment can be divided into five stages. I will discuss the first three in this chapter and the last two later.

Stage 1: "The world sucks." This is the bottom, the hopeless stage of life. It seems pointless to try. Employees stuck here are disengaged. The company would be better off if they were not employed.

Stage 2: "My life sucks." This is the *Dilbert* world, a world devoid of reciprocation, recognition or value.

A Stage 2 *company* has no purpose, vision or values. People in the company do not know how they contribute to the company and cannot explain costs or profit.

A Stage 2 *job* does not inspire and it does not have intrinsic rewards or autonomy. The job is a series of commands and instructions in a controlled environment.

A Stage 2 *boss* lacks emotional intelligence and does not believe employees can be trusted. This boss takes all the credit and ensures that blame flows downhill.

A Stage 2 *employee* has two modes: suck up and complain. These employees are passive-aggressive, antagonistic and adept at ensuring that downhill-flowing blame flows in someone else's direction. Customers are viewed as part of the problem. Employees in Stage 2 are not engaged.

. . . .

Stage 2: "My life sucks." This is the Dilbert *world, a world devoid of reciprocation, recognition or value.*

. . . .

Stage 3: "I'm great and you're not." Most people do not want to spend their lives working for a *Dilbert* boss. They want a career, not a job. There are three escape routes from Stage 2.

The first escape route is to get a *professional education*. Lawyers, accountants, engineers and doctors all have a great degree of autonomy. Professional work is not subject to detailed scrutiny and for the most part it supplies a stable, safe employment platform that pays fairly well.

The second escape route is to become an *expert at work*. An expert in the workplace is valuable and hard to replace. Experts can do favors and make the lives of other workers and bosses easier if they want. Experts have an unspoken perch of immunity in the workplace and are much less exposed to the fumblings of a Stage 2 boss.

The third escape route is to *start your own business*. Many businesses are started by strong, intelligent people so that they can do it their own way. The real motivation is a better lifestyle, free from a toxic, controlling workplace. These businesses are meant to provide a sense of freedom and escape. The intangible lifestyle considerations outweigh business considerations.

Each escape route – becoming a professional, an expert or a business owner – requires the strength of personality that says, "I'm great, you're not." Stage 3 personalities are intelligent, cynical and distrustful. They understand due diligence and don't often get scammed. Knowledge and expertise that nobody else has are very powerful and not easily shared.

There are frequent complaints from Stage 3 that others are not contributing enough or doing their share (because they are not great). People at Stage 3 believe it is easier to do things themselves because it takes too long to explain it to someone else. It is important to be in control of the conversation and to be the one who is right. Mistakes often result in a loss of temper.

In Stage 3, *partnerships* rarely work, agreements must be carefully documented and employees are not to be trusted. Control is very important because someone else will either mess up or take advantage.

Stage 3 *professionals* can group together in law firms or accounting firms but these firms are usually composed of independent rather than interdependent professionals. The purpose of the firm is to reduce overhead and provide referral opportunities. Compensation is measured in dollars and worth is measured in hourly rates and chargeable hours. The authors of *Tribal Leadership* explain:

> Professionals usually cap out at Stage Three. Attorneys, accountants, physicians, brokers, salespeople, are evaluated by what they know and do, and these measuring points are the hallmarks of Stage Three. "Teams" at this point mean a star and a supporting cast – surgeon and nurses, senior attorney or senior accountant and associates.

> Many of the people we interviewed at middle Stage Three work in knowledge-based organizations – medicine, the law, education, even politics. In each case, the person shows mild respect for others while promoting himself or herself as better.

> Each person wanted his or her profession to be the most important in the group; the consultants wanted the group to be known for consulting, and the account managers wanted everyone to focus on customer service. This disagreement – a hallmark of Stage Three – prevented them from forming a tribal identity: a requirement of Stage Four.

THE THREE CLASSIC ESCAPE ROUTES

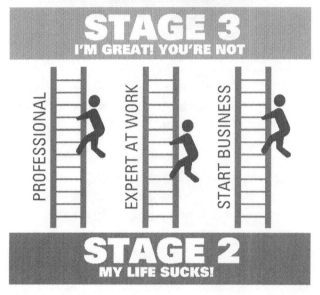

These are qualities of the Stage 3 business owner or professional:

» Prefers command and control over coaching
» Micromanages and does not empower the team
» Is not particularly interested in employees' success or personal well-being
» Is not particularly good at communicating – doesn't listen or share information

In writing this book it gradually occurred to me that the entire life-style business industry – owners, trusted advisors, accountants, lawyers, valuators – is for the most part stuck in Stage 3.

This systemic problem is caused by the "I'm great, you're not" attitude. This attitude leads to a lack of cooperation and collaboration that across hundreds of thousands of businesses leads to the macroeconomic problem CIBC called inadequate succession planning. It leads to value quicksand and it is the owner who is stuck. If you're stuck in Stage 3 it will be very hard to sell your business or to hire your buyer because all the knowledge, skills, control and value are tied to the owner. If you're the only one who's great, what happens to the business when you leave?

The Double Life

Jerry exemplifies a Stage 3 lifestyle business owner – all control and no trust. He had just returned from a month in Mexico, where he had celebrated his 60th birthday. His trucking business was doing quite well. Jerry had already talked to a business broker who explained that most of the value of the trucking business was in the trucks, land and building. Jerry had decided to work the business for 10 more years.

Bob, who was 30, ran the shop and the dispatch office. Bob did a great job and the employees liked him.

Jerry had never considered what would happen if Bob left. He didn't recognize Bob's contribution because after all, "I could do it better anyway." Jerry had never considered giving shares to Bob. "Why would I?" The accountant piped up, "It's a good idea; I've done it before. What you do is sell non-voting shares that you can buy back for a dollar. Every once in a while pay some dividends so he feels like an owner."

The accountant continued, warning, "You have to be careful – a lot of times lawyers mess things up, the employee goes for independent legal advice and that lawyer starts asking for voting rights and access to financial information." Jerry perked up. "Financial information? I don't see why we should do that." The employee share idea was dropped.

Jerry's problem was that he had bargained with his employees for lower wages by crying poor. But in Mexico Jerry had a nice condo and a 36-foot boat. He never told his employees about the condo or the boat because he figured they'd want more money.

Many lifestyle business owners lead this kind of double life. Control becomes increasingly important in these situations. Where the double life really catches up with you is when you have to consider business succession. The lack of trust in the employees largely eliminates the possibility of working with them to take over the business and the high level of control the owner has exercised substantially decreases the transferability and value of the business.

The Transactional Approach: "Prove It to Me"

True succession planning is a long-term process. One of its challenges is the transactional way in which most professionals work. Most competent lawyers and accountants view their practices as a series of discrete transactions – the sale of a business, a real estate deal, a tax return, an audit, a lawsuit.

Both the pricing and the parameters of what is expected in transaction work are well established. The lawyer and the accountant know what they are going to deliver and clients know what they are going to get. In many cases the process of the transaction is so routine that almost the entire transaction is handled by a clerk or an associate who does not have a professional license. Often transaction work is a commodity for which the client's only concern is price.

Transactions are generally one-time events between people who don't know each other and who will not be working together again. The great legal and accounting engine in North America processes hundreds of millions of transactions every year with hardly a peep of complaint.

Transaction work is based on the premise of "prove it to me." A vigilant eye is kept open for fraudulent dealing. Lawyers and accountants would be negligent if they did not obtain confirming documentation for each step in the transaction process. Transactions are not based on trust. It is negligent to trust in a transaction.

In the sale of a business each element and aspect of the business is subject to proof. The process is called due diligence; trust is not required or expected. It would be negligent for a lawyer or an auditor to trust the word of someone from the business being investigated. It would be unprofessional for someone from that business to ask a lawyer or auditor to trust them. Trust has no place in a legal transaction.

The largest and most lucrative transactions are large-business acquisitions or divestitures. A substantial industry of M&A professionals, investment bankers and huge law and accounting firms has developed to perform the due diligence and closing of large-business transactions. The primary attraction of large-transaction work is the large amount of money exchanged on closing – consulting fees can run into the hundreds of millions of dollars.

The business transaction industry has written books, taught courses and built firms on the standards and practices that have developed for successful large transactions. A lot of transaction wisdom has been developed, including these points:

» Keep everything confidential.
» Don't tell your employees.
» Don't sell to employees unless they have skin in the game (that is, will pay money at closing).
» Buying and selling a business is an adversarial process.
» Due diligence has to be exercised to prove every aspect of the transaction.

This orthodoxy has permeated the thinking of almost every professional who views business transactions or succession files. What the players and observers of these transactions don't appreciate is that none of these points have intrinsic merit. They simply reflect standards of practice that have developed in the transaction sector. Lest you think I am fluffy-headed when I cast aspersions on transaction wisdom, consider this question: given the steely eyed determination with which the mega-fee transactions are carried out, what do you think the success rate is for these rational, due-diligence-driven deals?

The answer is astounding.

According to *Forbes* magazine and *Harvard Business Review*, study after study has confirmed that more than 50% of M&A transactions fail. McKinsey, the world's largest consulting company, says, "Most mergers are doomed from the beginning. Anyone who has researched merger success rates knows that roughly 70 percent of mergers fail."

· · · · · · · · · · · · · · ·

M&A failure is not a failure of due diligence or reason and logic; it is a failure on the people side of the business – a failure of "soft issues."

· · · · · · · · · · · · · · ·

By failure they mean that the investment does not achieve the rate of return that was expected, or worse. America Online (AOL) was the first large Internet search service. In 2000 AOL acquired Time-Warner for $165 billion. This merger was a cultural disaster – the old-school Time-Warner management and the non-conformist software engineers of AOL clashed. Talented employees left in droves. Two years later AOL recorded a $99 billion loss, at the time the largest corporate loss in history and as of this writing less than $1 billion behind the 2008 losses at AIG. It is unlikely that anyone even considered asking the advisors for a refund.

The two biggest reasons M&A transactions fail are cultural incompatibility and lack of management depth. M&A failure is not a failure of due diligence or reason and logic; it is a failure on the people side of the business – a failure of "soft issues." As we'll discuss later, it is mastery of these very issues that builds greatness and through greatness, value.

Are Lawyers Really Better Off at the Bottom of the Ocean?

Many people like to blame lawyers and their hostile attitudes for the failure of business deals. This is an issue for owners because every business succession requires legal documentation and the lawyer can play a very important role.

Mark McCormack was a good enough golfer to qualify for the US Open. He also made it through Yale law school. After working for a few years as a lawyer he founded International Management Group (IMG), a sports and entertainment agency, in 1960. His first big client was golfer Arnold Palmer. McCormack is credited with professionalizing the business side of sports and developing the modern concept of athletic endorsements.

McCormack wrote a number of bestsellers. One was called *The Terrible Truth about Lawyers*, which included this: "It's the lawyers who (1) gum up the works; (2) get people mad at each other; (3) make business procedures more expensive than they need to be; and (4) now and then deep-six what had seemed like a perfectly workable arrangement."

McCormack further observed that, "When lawyers try to horn in on the business aspects of a deal, the practical result is usually confusion and wasted time." He concluded, "the best way to deal with lawyers is not to deal with them at all." McCormack thought lawyers were trained to find problems, not solve them.

Most lawyers have heard stories like this and are often confused by them. This is not how they see themselves at all. They see themselves as protecting their clients. Even the governing bodies are self-conscious about this issue. Surveys by the Law Society of Upper Canada confirm that while people may "hate" lawyers generally they almost always like their own lawyer.

This is so because lawyers are trained to represent the interests of their client to the exclusion of others. The cardinal rule for lawyers is that they avoid conflicts of interest, and conflicts of interest arise when we consider the interests of others. This is the wording from the *Ontario Rules of Professional Conduct* for lawyers:

> The lawyer has a duty to the client to raise fearlessly every issue, advance every argument, and ask every question, however distasteful, which the lawyer thinks will help the client's case and to endeavour to obtain for the client the benefit of every remedy and defence authorized by law.

This idea of fearlessly representing the owner's interest is a real problem in a hire your buyer situation. When you hire your buyer you have to take everyone's interests into account and many lawyers simply can't do that.

When a client hands a problem to a lawyer, often the only hammer the lawyer has is litigation. McCormack observed that two CEOs can often resolve a dispute inexpensively over lunch in an hour or two when teams of lawyers couldn't do it in months or even years. McCormack's observations are valid but he does not identify the cause of the problem.

What both McCormack and the lawyers are missing is the distinction between transactions where there is no ongoing relationship and no need for trust, and long-term business relationships, where there *is* a need for trust.

McCormack was missing the fact that those two CEOs are able to resolve issues over lunch because they trust each other. Lawyers are professionally disabled: they *cannot* trust each other; every fact and every document requires proof.

Lawyers are not really better off at the bottom of the ocean (although I am a strong swimmer). But they would be better off if they appreciated that the rational, no-trust "prove it to me" approach that works so well in hundreds of millions of transactions every year gums up the works in long-term business relationships. And to hire your buyer you need to develop a trusting, long-term relationship.

The Trouble with Trusted Advisors: The "Silly Debate"

Most small business owners have just one truly trusted professional advisor they tend to go to for their professional issues. This trusted relationship may be formed with an accountant, a lawyer or a financial advisor. As one really good small business lawyer said to me, "I'm really a generalist in patent law, securities law, tax law, insurance law, mergers and a dozen other areas. I know who to call and my clients trust me to do that."

Accounting societies, banks and insurance companies understand this and urge their members to become "trusted advisors." The advantage of occupying the trusted advisor chair is that you control client engagements. This arrangement is valuable for the advisor and the institution but leads to the "silly debate": "I do your taxes, so it's me"; "No, I lend you money, so it's me"; "No, no, I build your wealth, so it's me." All "I'm great, you're not" – no team, no collaboration.

The trouble with trusted advisors arises when they operate from a Stage 3 perspective. No doubt you want an "I'm great" professional on your team. It's the "you're not" that you have to watch for. Professionals who believe *their* profession is the most important, and who show little respect for other service providers, can do a great deal of harm.

Some professionals use trusted advisor status to put a fence around you. Accountants often tell you not to make an important financial decision without reviewing it with them. This is valuable advice if your accountant is an expert at everything, but in this day and age no one can be. But the trusted advisor fallacy can lead into this trap.

Consider the client who just sold a business for $55 million. What should they do? Many turn to their trusted accountant for advice. But is an accountant genuinely an investment expert? Is it sufficient for the accountant to refer the client to the accountant's own wealth advisor? Has that wealth advisor handled accounts that size? The appropriate advice is to interview two or three investment firms to get an objective view of what's available.

This brings us to the entire question of referrals. Referrals are very important. In many cases they work out very well and you know you are being referred to someone you can trust. But you should be aware that referrals can be very lucrative – to the referrer. In many law firms the lawyer who makes the referral gets one-third of the fee that the client actually pays – without doing any work on the file.

Trusted advisors are essential, but to be truly trusted the advisors have to honestly recognize their own professional limitations. The trusted advisor fallacy arises when the client believes a professional is an expert in all types of professional advice. Many professionals encourage this thinking, suggesting that if it is important the professional will take care of it.

When we ask about succession planning we often hear "my accountant takes care of that." The reality is often different – the accountant may have mentioned the words but nothing has happened and the discussion keeps getting postponed "until next year." I even heard one senior accountant from a respected firm say that "business succession is either about selling the business or dealing with an emergency situation" with no comprehension or concern that there may be other options.

An additional complicating factor is that most outstanding lawyers and accountants are extremely busy. "I'm swamped" is professional code for "I'm great." Even if we ignore the Stage 3 bias that no one else is important, some professionals are so busy that they simply cannot come up for air long enough to consider the in-depth type of work that good succession planning demands.

There is even a professional bias against employees. Many professionals view employees as somehow less worthy of consideration. When I mention the hire your buyer idea I'm often asked, "but who will run the company?" as if somehow a person who is or was an employee is not capable of doing so.

So for all these reasons owners need to have a balanced, objective view of the capabilities and limitations of their existing advisors.

Litigation: The Lose-Lose Game

The last impediment that professionals face in the soft skills, engagement and trust approach is that their entire frame of reference, their viewpoint, is grounded in the litigation system.

When a business is sold, the buyer gets a book with dozens of numbered tabs containing different legal agreements and confirmations answering different inquiries in the due diligence process. All of these legal agreements and confirmations are based on requirements developed by common law. Common law is based on precedents. Precedents are decisions that resulted from court cases. What this means is that the structure and approach of the law is forged in the furnace of litigation.

If there is ever a problem with a business agreement the legal procedure for fixing it is litigation. The theory makes sense – where there is a difference of opinion about an agreement or if one side is not honoring the agreement, a judge should review the dispute and issue a ruling that fixes the problem.

For simple transactions such as a mortgage or the sale of a car, the litigation system can be quite effective. For long-term business relationships, however, the litigation process is terrible.

Let's look at two cases that serve as cautionary tales about the probable outcomes when litigation is used to manage a complex business relationship.

The first case, involving Rosa Becker, is one of the most significant family law cases in Canadian history. Rosa Becker established the legal precedent that common law spouses can make a claim against a family business that they do not own.

Rosa Becker and Lothar Pettkus were immigrants to Canada; they met in 1955. They moved in together but did not marry or have children. Lothar used his own money to buy a beekeeping farm and registered it in his own name. Rosa was hardworking and shared the farm labor with Lothar for 20 years.

In 1971, Lothar purchased another property with profits from the beekeeping operation and money from his own bank account. The family beekeeping business now had two valuable pieces of land, both owned by Lothar. In 1974, Rosa and Lothar separated.

Rosa sued Lothar for half of the beekeeping business. The law at that time was that a common law spouse was not legally entitled to a share in any property or business owned by the other common law spouse.

Six years after Rosa launched her suit the Supreme Court of Canada released its decision. The court said it was reasonable for Rosa to expect to get something for her 20 years of labor on the farm. Lothar had freely accepted the benefits of her labor knowing that Rosa expected to be treated fairly. The court held that it would be unjust to allow Lothar to keep everything and awarded Rosa a 50% share of the beekeeping business.

Rosa's case became quite famous. The new way of sharing family businesses between common law spouses became law in several Canadian provinces and in other places in the world as far away as Australia.

Sadly, in the end Rosa got nothing from her six-year investment in the lawsuit. Lothar refused to pay anything. He sold the beekeeping business, spent most of the money and then went bankrupt. The money that was left went to Rosa's lawyers for their fees. In a tragic turn of events, Rosa committed suicide in 1986. Her suicide note accused the legal system of forcing her hand.

The reality is that courts can provide little assistance when a person is determined to ensure that you lose even if it means they themselves have to lose in the process.

Our second case is about spreadsheet software. VisiCalc, developed by a company called Software Arts, was the first spreadsheet software. It was released in 1979 for the Apple II. It was so popular that the term "killer application" was invented to describe it. The killer part was that people would spend $100 for VisiCalc and then spend another $2,000 for an Apple II so they could run it.

To land the Apple deal, Software Arts entered a distribution agreement with a company that would become VisiCorp. The relationship between Software Arts and VisiCorp was never good; the owners of the two firms frequently argued. This lack of cooperation and acrimony resulted in very poor follow-through.

In 1980 IBM was ready to launch the first personal computer (PC) to compete with Apple. IBM was very concerned that the 1979 VisiCalc program written for the Apple operating system was gaining serious traction. IBM asked VisiCalc to write a version of VisiCalc for the PC. At the time VisiCalc was such a dominant force in the new personal computing industry that IBM did not even publicly announce that it would be selling the PC until the PC version of VisiCalc was ready. IBM delayed the launch of the PC a full year until 1981 waiting for VisiCalc.

Over at VisiCalc, the real reason for the IBM delay was the frequent arguments and acrimony between Software Arts and VisiCorp. Within a year of the IBM PC launch both companies took the accusations public and an eager press spread the word. The situation went from bad to worse.

The IBM PC was a tremendous success. Software Arts quickly grew to $50 million in value and planned an initial public offering of its shares for the fall of 1983. Software Arts was also planning to end its relationship with VisiCorp now that it was big enough not to need it.

Meanwhile, in the background, a company called Lotus was working diligently on a competing spreadsheet program called Lotus 1-2-3.

In September 1983, as Software Arts was planning to go public, VisiCorp launched a $60 million lawsuit. VisiCorp alleged that Software Arts was holding back on upgrades to VisiCalc until it went public, when it planned to end its relationship with VisiCorp. Software Arts hit back with a lawsuit claiming that VisiCorp had been launching other "Visi" products at the expense of VisiCalc. The war was on – senior executives of both companies boarded up with lawyers for months on end preparing evidence, affidavits and documents. It was one of the biggest and most expensive lawsuits in the computer industry to that point in history.

Late in 1983 Lotus launched a version of Lotus 1-2-3 with many of the upgrades that VisiCalc had been promising. Lotus wasted no time in taking advantage of the hole in the market created by the distractions of immense litigation swirling around VisiCalc.

By September 1984 both sides were spent – literally: all the money was gone and little was coming in. The *New York Times* reported,

> One of the most bitterly fought lawsuits in the personal computer industry, pitting the company that developed the once-popular VisiCalc program against the company that held the rights to market it, was settled out of court yesterday.
>
> Analysts said that the suit, which went on for a year as sales of VisiCalc slumped, appeared to end in a draw.
>
> "We decided that lawsuits just don't make sense," said Julian Lange, the president of Software Arts.

VisiCalc had already lost more than 90% of the market to Lotus 1-2-3. Six months later, in the spring of 1985, Software Arts filed for bankruptcy protection. Lotus picked up the assets of Software Arts, including VisiCalc, for next to nothing in a liquidation sale. Shortly afterward VisiCorp was purchased by another software company.

The worldview of lawyers and accountants is deeply affected by the litigation process. Lawyers see the bad cases: the partnerships that fail, the marriages that collapse and the employees who sue. This constant refrain of litigation and hostility makes lawyers very alert and very cynical. It also makes it very difficult for them to trust because they have seen it all before.

This thinking leads lawyers to recommend against partnerships and shareholders. Lawyers often insist that owners maintain as much control as they can. They view employees and children with suspicion and actually tell their clients that they cannot carry out certain transactions. In one case, a lawyer refused to allow the owner's son into the business until the son's wife signed a postnuptial agreement. She refused. The whole thing caused a lot of family problems and succession planning was delayed for 10 years.

Interestingly, it would surprise most lawyers if you pointed out one of their professional practices – taking the position that it's negligent to advise an owner to "trust" an employee, partner or shareholder. Like fish in water, lawyers are simply too immersed in the "prove it to me" approach to be aware of it – or its detrimental impact. In the legal world trust is replaced by contract terms and penalties. The false promise of these terms and penalties is that they provide superior solutions to any problems that may arise.

A commonly held view among judges and senior lawyers is that a good settlement is one in which both sides are upset. The wisdom in that statement is that when both sides are upset it seems unlikely that one side is taking advantage of the other. But what does that say about the goals of the system? The goal of the system is to have both sides walk away upset. In other words, lose-lose is the expectation of the justice system.

It does not take a lot of introspection to realize there may be a better way.

In the next chapter I set out the evidence for a better way for businesspeople to conduct themselves so they can set the stage for the creation of value and avoid having to fall back on the justice system.

Chapter 4

The Search for Value: Lessons from the World's Best

How Do You Create Value?

IF YOU ASKED PEOPLE how to create value in a business most would assume that value relates to some type of financial formula. There is a formula: free cash flow times a multiple, but no matter how many times you press the button or kick the console on that formula, nothing happens. The formula by itself is barren and inert. What you need is power to light it up. That power is engagement. Engagement arises out of simple human courtesies, trust and emotional intelligence. This chapter explores these issues. The first issue relates to the myths and incorrect assumptions many advisors make.

Myths about Children and Employees

A lot of articles and tips on succession planning contain helpful advice based on common sense. There are many articles that discuss whether family members should be invited into the family business. It is as if simply saying "never gift shares to children" or "children have to earn their way into the business" is enough to make it true in all situations. Similar things are said about employees – that they must have skin in the game or that they are not entrepreneurial enough to run a business and so on.

It is not that these articles are wrong; they definitely contain wisdom based on experience. The problem is that the writers assume that the one experience is true in all situations. It can equally be said that children who grow up in a family business have a depth of knowledge and experience that cannot be duplicated. Many child prodigies grew up in the family business: Mozart's father was a composer, Picasso's an art professor. Howard Hughes took over the family business at age 18 after his father died, and Tom Watson Jr. was considered an irresponsible college kid while his father was alive, but then built IBM into the world's most valuable company in the 20 years after his father died.

The story of Gordon Getty is an example of how far off base common succession advice can be. Getty Oil was founded by J. Paul Getty. In the late 1950s, *Fortune* magazine described J. Paul as the richest person in America.

J. Paul had four sons. Three of them self-destructed, largely as a result of the stress of being the sons of J. Paul Getty. George, the eldest, was very able in business. He worked his way up to the number two spot in the company behind his father. But the stress of dealing with his father's constant badgering became too much for him; he committed suicide at the age of 48.

J. Paul's second son, Ronald, had worked at Getty Oil, but after he made some errors in judgment, George convinced their father to fire him.

Another son, Eugene Paul, who later changed his name to J. Paul Getty Jr., also started out at Getty Oil, but he too ran into problems and was fired. He joined the international jet set, but with an unlimited budget he overdid the party life and became addicted to drugs.

Gordon, the fourth son, became a professional musician who wrote and conducted operas. Neither his father nor the management of Getty Oil took him seriously – he was viewed as far too soft for the harsh realities of the oil patch and had never shown any aptitude for business. A self-described "absent-minded professor," Gordon had been forced to leave Getty Oil (again at George's insistence) after a series of unfortunate incidents, one of them involving his failure to remember what he had done with a company car.

Gordon's accidental rise to power stemmed from the fates of his brothers and from a trust that his grandmother had set up that owned the family shares of Getty Oil. She created the trust so that on its termination all the assets would be distributed to J. Paul's children or their descendants. In the meantime, only the income from the trust would be available to the family members.

Before J. Paul died, he appointed three trustees to manage the trust when he died: Gordon, who by then J. Paul considered the least incompetent of his surviving children; Lansing Hays, J. Paul's longtime lawyer and right-hand man; and Security Pacific National Bank, then the second-largest bank in California.

When J. Paul died in 1976 the bank refused to serve as trustee, passing up a $3 million a year fee for fear of the potential liability. Getty Oil was a tough, nasty organization and the value of the trust was so large that a judgment for mismanaging it could destroy the bank. This meant that when Hays died in 1982, Gordon was left in sole charge of the trust, which owned 40% of the stock of Getty Oil Company.

When Gordon started to investigate the process of selling the shares of Getty Oil he found that the shares were substantially undervalued. Gordon could not get a fair offer because no one in the industry would take him seriously.

In 1982 the shares were valued at about $50 per share and were in danger of falling further if something wasn't done. This was a deeply discounted value – Getty Oil had proven oil reserves worth at least $100 per share.

Gordon took the seemingly naive route of discussing confidential company information with notorious corporate raider T. Boone Pickens. Pickens, also a Texan, had attacked many weak companies, dismantling and selling them at a great profit. The Getty board of directors and the Getty lawyers were furious and very vocal about Gordon's lapse of judgment.

Thus began one of the ugliest corporate battles in history. In December 1983 Gordon got word that Pennzoil was interested in Getty's oil reserves. A deal was agreed to in January 1984. The deal was that together, Gordon Getty and Pennzoil would buy the rest of the Getty Oil shares and Pennzoil would operate Getty Oil. The price would be $110 per share.

The board demanded that Pennzoil sweeten its offer, which it did, by $5 per share; the board then signed a memorandum of understanding with Pennzoil. The board did not seem to appreciate that the memorandum of understanding could be considered binding. Immediately after the meeting the board sought competitive offers.

Two days later Texaco made an offer of $125 per share for a total takeover price of $10 billion. At the time this was the largest takeover in history. Gordon asked Texaco for an indemnity against any lawsuits by Pennzoil and promptly sold the trust shares for $4 billion (40% of $10 billion).

Pennzoil sued Texaco. Pennzoil claimed that Texaco wrongfully interfered with the deal Pennzoil had made with the board of Getty Oil. Pennzoil took its case to a Texas jury. Texaco brought in a famous New York lawyer who testified that the memorandum of understanding was not binding. Pennzoil's lawyer addressed the jury, "Well I'm not sure how those smooth talkin' lawyers operate in New York City, but here in Texas when a man makes a deal he keeps it." The jury agreed, resulting in the largest civil verdict to that point in history: $10.3 billion. Texaco, one of the largest oil companies in the world at the time, had to declare bankruptcy.

What are the facts here?

- » One of the most valuable companies in the world
- » A hyper-competitive industry swarming with corporate raiders and litigation lawyers
- » A father who was the world's richest man
- » Three siblings destroyed by the family business
- » The largest, ugliest takeover in history
- » The largest civil verdict in history
- » One of the world's largest oil companies going bankrupt
- » All managed by a "least likely to succeed" musician

What advice would you have given J. Paul about the trust? Let me guess: incentive provisions? What advice would you have given the other beneficiaries of the trust? How about Gordon? Let's look at the judgment of history.

In October 1984 *Forbes* announced that Gordon Getty was the richest man in America, reporting that he had received $4 billion for shares that had a market value of $1.6 billion a little more than a year earlier.

Each of Gordon's apparent missteps, such as "naively" talking to corporate raider Pickens, appears in retrospect to have been a carefully orchestrated step leading to a historic outcome. His clever use of the fact that people laughed behind his back, misjudging his strength, is a classic strategy straight out of *The Art of War*.

What skill was it that allowed Gordon to walk unscathed through this valley of death? Gordon claims that it was music that helped him "dodge the curse" his inheritance brought. An example of Gordon's emotional maturity was the fact that a year later he was no longer a billionaire. *Forbes* reported that his fortune had dropped by more than 75% because he had distributed equal shares to his siblings' families.

The point of Gordon's story is that following standard advice would have produced a very different outcome. Every situation is different and it is really up to you to create the succession plan that makes sense in your situation.

Stage 4: "We're Great"

We have reviewed *Tribal Leadership*'s first three stages. Let's continue with Stage 4. It is literally impossible to do business *succession* with just you and your advisors because you have to transfer the business to someone. Thinking about the business in terms of "we" is required. Thinking in "we" means moving to Stage 4: "We're great."

Stage 4 involves the development of engaged employees who can function without supervision and are thus much better suited for succession. In business succession we cannot afford to have the place fall apart when we leave. Instead what we are trying to do is develop a team that can build on the foundation and drive five to 10 times more value out of the company than was there before we started.

If you have concerns that you are, or were, a Stage 3 leader, don't worry. The authors of *Tribal Leadership* argue that you must go through Stage 3 – "I'm great" – before you can get to Stage 4, "We're great."

A Stage 4 *company* has purpose, vision and values. People in the company know why the company exists. They know how they contribute to the company and can explain costs and profit.

A Stage 4 *career* inspires and has intrinsic rewards and autonomy. The career is self-motivating, with employees left to do the work in an uncontrolled environment.

A Stage 4 *leader* is emotionally intelligent and trusts the team. A Stage 4 leader does not take the credit and ensures that employees are protected from accusation and blame.

A Stage 4 *employee* has two modes: speak up about problems and work toward solutions. Employees at this stage attack problems aggressively, support their peers and are adept at ensuring that recognition and appreciation flow in many directions. They view customer service as a priority. Employees in Stage 4 are engaged, trusting and trustworthy. They believe that the sum of an engaged group effort is greater than a multiple of the parts. They believe in win-win and look forward to going to work.

. . . .

Thinking about the business in terms of "we" is required.
Thinking in "we" means moving to Stage 4: "We're great."

. . . .

Moving to Stage 4 can be part of a very effective solution for lifestyle business owners stuck in a Stage 3 world. If you can't sell your business, hire your buyer. The reason I say "hire" is that the person who becomes your buyer has to qualify for that position. In addition, and somewhat less obvious, is the fact that you as the owner also have to qualify. You have to move yourself and your employees to Stage 4.

Stage 5: "The World Is Great"

There is also a Stage 5. In *Tribal Leadership* the authors talk about some of the world's best companies. These companies seem to have moved beyond the level of a successful "We're great" company to a stage removed – companies such as Apple and Amgen, which makes cancer drugs. These companies have so much impact they change the world. Although I don't want to discourage you from changing the world, in terms of business succession planning it is sufficient that you change your own world.

How Google Made Its Case

I really like this story about the lesson Google learned about management. It is a universal lesson that will help you move into a "we're great" culture.

It is easy to see how people working at Google – a company with a value of $248 billion in 2014, employing the best and the brightest – could easily believe "I'm great, you're not." And indeed they did.

Googlers believed in technology, not management. They thought management was a bureaucratic fussiness that got in the way of real work. In short, Google was a lifestyle company for brilliant technical people who wanted cutting-edge work. Most lifestyle business owners share this disdain for management.

Harvard professor David A. Garvin described the Google lifestyle in a *Harvard Business Review* article, "How Google Sold Its Engineers on Management." He notes that from the company's inception, Google had been dubious about the need for managers. The company comprised a group of engineers, who naturally wanted to spend their time designing software, not reporting and supervising. "In their hearts they've long believed that management is more destructive than beneficial, a distraction from 'real work' and tangible, goal-directed tasks." Garvin describes what happened when Google took the notion of working without managers to its ultimate expression:

> A few years into the company's life, founders Larry Page and Sergey Brin actually wondered whether Google needed any managers at all. In 2002 they experimented with a completely flat organization, eliminating engineering managers in an effort to break down barriers to rapid idea development and to replicate the collegial environment they'd enjoyed in graduate school. That experiment lasted only a few months: They relented when too many people went directly to Page (a multi-billionaire) with questions about expense reports, interpersonal conflicts, and other nitty-gritty issues.

Even though Google made number one on the *Fortune* 100 Best Employers list for 2007 and 2008 it was worried about employee retention. Google may be the world's fifth most valuable brand but unlike number three, Coca-Cola, Google has a constantly evolving product that relies on the smarts and intuition of its people to keep it on top.

Dominance in technology can be lost quickly. Employee retention is important for companies like Google, and it's equally important for lifestyle business owners who want to hire a buyer as part of a comprehensive succession plan.

In 2008 Google human resources set up a private Google Group to ask former employees why they left the company. The results revealed, with brutal honesty, what it's like to work at Google, at least from the point of view of employees who were unhappy enough to resign. Top among the complaints was low pay relative to what they could earn elsewhere and disappearing fringe benefits. Other consistent complaints were that there was too much bureaucracy, poor management and poor mentoring.

Google was surprised by the results. It was coming to be viewed as a place to get training, not a place to stay. Google realized that a great company is more than a collection of great engineers. Management *did* matter but no one was sure what good management was.

Google set out to prove what elements of management would work for it. The method of proof was based on the same data-crunching principles that made Google great in the first place. A team of PhDs was hired and tasked with proving that management mattered. The team applied the same analytical rigor and tools that were used in other aspects of Google's business.

The list of management behaviors that the team discovered is surprising at first because it's so basic. On reflection, the list makes perfect sense. If you are a brilliant young engineer living in an "I'm great and you're not unless you design algorithms" world, common sense is often crushed under the weight of complex code. Simple human courtesies are viewed as weaknesses that get in the way of a higher technical mission. The same problem arises in the legal and accounting professions – technically brilliant people working in high-pressure environments without time to pause or reflect on simple human courtesies.

These are the first three of the eight simple truths discovered by the most brilliant of the world's technicians.

A good Google manager

1. Is a good coach
2. Empowers the team and does not micromanage
3. Expresses interest in and concern for team members' success and personal well-being

Although these qualities sound quaint and suited more for an entry-level college management course, in a fast-paced business environment their very simplicity belies their value. These qualities are precisely the inverse of the qualities displayed at Stage 3. These are Stage 4 qualities. Coaching, empowerment, interest and concern – sounds like engagement! They work for Google and they will help you build value too.

The Best Employers Outperform

It's all well and good to talk about employee engagement and trust but if you wanted to invest in the stock market, what measure would you look at? Isn't *return on investment* what we're looking for? So how do the ideas of employee engagement and trust stand up to strict investor criteria?

Every year *Fortune* magazine publishes a list of the 100 Best Employers. The list is compiled by a company called the Great Place to Work Institute based on surveys of over 10 million employees every year. Best employers are noted for having the highest levels of employee engagement.

The financial performance of the 100 Best Employers was compared to that of the s&p 500 to see how these companies measured up. To be sure any given year's results were not a fluke, the comparison was made for every year from 1997 to 2013. The results surprised me: the 100 Best Employers *outperform the stock market average by almost 2 to 1*. From 1997 to 2013 the *Fortune* 100 Best Employers had an average return of 11.80%. The s&p 500 had an average return of 6.04% over the same period. Bottom line: employee engagement builds value.

Long-Term Business Relationships: As Deep as Trust

We've looked at the evidence that confirms that *employee engagement* is actually a superior business practice that generates a significantly higher return on investment, but where does *trust* fit in?

The 100 Best Employers list is based on surveys of two to three million employees per year, testing for the qualities that make for the best employer. Since 1997, the first year of the list, the number one quality of the best employers by a large margin, according to their own employees, has been *trust*.

Long-term business relationships are as deep and as valuable as the trust that binds them. The very depth of a business relationship is measured by the trust it generates. A lawyer will advise you not to trust and that you should rely on detailed contracts with penalty clauses to maintain control, but there is abundant evidence that good business relationships are based on trust, not penalties.

. . . .

Best employers are noted for having the highest levels of employee engagement. The 100 Best Employers **outperform the stock market average by almost 2 to 1.**

. . . .

When I was a young lawyer I spoke with a vice president at a large robotics company. He had just signed a contract worth several hundred million dollars. I asked if he had a lawyer look at it and he said, "Why would I do that? It's only two pages long and I know what it says. Besides, it doesn't matter what it says, we don't really know all of the problems that will come up so we have to work it out as we go." Given the sizes of the companies and the contracts involved, litigation was out of the question.

This was very perplexing to me because it went against everything I had learned. I was concerned that my friend would be exposed to all kinds of dangers without "proper legal protection." But when he asked, "What protection?" I was unable to articulate anything that would be helpful. At the time I was too deeply entrenched as a lawyer to realize that when there is very significant value at stake the parties simply cannot afford to rely on legal language and litigation.

Stephen M.R. Covey wrote *The Speed of Trust.* The idea is that where you have trust you have speed; where you don't have trust you have grind. Covey explains the feeling of trust:

> Think of a person with whom you have a high trust relationship – perhaps a boss, co-worker, customer, spouse, parent, sibling, child, or friend. Describe this relationship. What's it like? How does it feel? How well do you communicate? How quickly can you get things done? How much do you enjoy this relationship?

> Now think of a person with whom you have a low-trust relationship... How is the communication? Does it flow quickly and freely... or do you feel like you're constantly walking on land mines and being misunderstood? Do you work together to get

things done quickly... or does it take a disproportionate amount of time and energy to finally reach agreement and execution? Do you enjoy this relationship... or do you find it tedious, cumbersome, and draining?

Covey referred to the McLane deal as an example of the speed of trust. In 2002 Berkshire Hathaway bought McLane Distribution from Walmart for $1.45 billion. Warren Buffett, principal of Berkshire Hathaway, has had a long-term, trusting relationship with Walmart executives.

Buffett described the deal in Berkshire Hathaway's annual report: "To make the McLane deal, we had a single meeting of about two hours. We then shook hands. Twenty-nine days later, Walmart had their money. We did no due diligence. We knew everything would be exactly the way Walmart said it would be, and it was."

A deal this size would normally take up to a year. The amount spent on legal and transaction fees could run to $50 million and internal management would expend enormous effort. If Buffett had been misled by the Walmart executives he could have been fired for negligence.

Trust is a cornerstone of Buffett's investment strategy. When he buys a new business, he places his trust in the executives of the company he is taking over. Buffett buys only companies with executives he wants to keep and then leaves them alone – trusting them to make money for Berkshire Hathaway. Buffett's headquarters staff is only about 20 people, who oversee 77 operating companies and 257,000 employees, a sign of the trust in the leaders of those companies. Clearly, for Warren Buffett trust builds value.

The "Trust Dividend": The Role of Contracts in Long-Term Relationships

A lawyer sees a business as a fabric sewn together with contracts. The concept of operating without a contract seems heretical. Contracts are very useful in one-time or short-term transactions, but what is the role of contracts in long-term business relationships?

This is an important question. When you hire your buyer you are not simply completing a transaction, you are engaging in a long-term business strategy that has a long-term relationship at its core. But how can we get reliable guidance on the parameters of such a relationship?

Fortunately we do not have to guess. The role of contracts in outsourcing relationships was studied for 21 years. Outsourcing relationships provide near-perfect specimens to study the role of contracts because they are significant semi-permanent business relationships.

Outsourcing is very common in the information technology (IT) field and the contracts can be very large and critically important to the client. In 2013 IT outsourcing was estimated to generate $288 billion by the IT research and advisory firm Gartner. In 2007 IT outsourcing firm Logica published a white paper, in association with the London School of Economics, entitled "The Outsourcing Enterprise: The Power of Relationships." The purpose of the study was to bring precision to the elements of a successful outsourcing relationship.

Logica studied 1,200 outsourcing relationships over a 21-year timeframe. Outsourcing, they found, should not be viewed as a transaction. The real issue is how you generate a successful relationship: "Successful relationships do not just happen."

Business relationships fall along a spectrum from power-based to trust-based. Power-based relationships are governed by contract terms and enforced by penalties. The study found that unless the contract was short term, power-based relationships were poor substitutes for trust-based relationships. The problem is the "high transaction costs of monitoring and imposing sanctions, the negative orientations and behaviors adopted, and the limited goals that can be pursued by the parties."

The study found, in contrast, that "good relationship management made a 40% difference in cost savings." The authors refer to this 40% cost savings as the "trust dividend."

Significantly, in a related study of 231 companies none cited a good contract as a key factor. Good relationship management techniques, such as flexible working arrangements, willingness to change and frequent and effective communication, were regularly mentioned.

However, the study pointed out that contracts do play an important role. They are necessary to form the outlines and parameters of what is expected of both parties. Both parties to the contract need to profit from the relationship and how that is done needs to be spelled out. Poorly drafted contracts based on faulty assumptions and containing flaws, ambiguities and loopholes can lead to serious relationship damage. They concluded that contracts form the foundation, but that they are an "insufficient governance tool." Governance is best managed through a good relationship.

A key insight about business relationships is that "you regularly hit what you aim at." The authors suggest that the parties develop a *relationship values charter*. This charter is a clear statement of the values or principles that the parties will use to govern the ongoing relationship. Examples of values from a relationship value charter include the following:

» Communication: We will communicate frequently, openly and honestly with each other.
» Meeting needs: We will both be proactive and reactive to each other's needs.
» Conflict: We recognize conflict as natural and will focus on solving the problem, not apportioning blame. We will resolve conflict at the lowest level.
» External relations: We will project a united front and will not discuss sensitive issues outside the relationship.

These relationship values, not contract penalties, drive superior performance and the 40% cost saving trust dividend.

TRUST DIVIDEND

LONG-TERM
BUSINESS
RELATIONSHIPS

40%

INCREASE IN
COST SAVINGS

There is a school of thought that contracts can be harmful in certain situations. When Pixar and Disney merged, Pixar had an unbroken string of hits and Disney had not had a hit in 16 years. Disney executives expressed concern during merger negotiations that Pixar had no employment agreements. Disney was afraid the Pixar creative team could just walk away after the deal. Ed Catmull, president of Pixar, explains his view of employment contracts in his book *Creativity, Inc.*

My feeling about employment contracts is that they hurt the employee and the employer.

The contracts in question were one-sided in favor of the studio, resulting in unexpected negative consequences. First and foremost, there was no longer any effective feedback between bosses and employees. If someone had a problem with the company, there wasn't much point in complaining because they were under contract. If someone didn't perform well, on the other hand, there was no point in confronting them about it; their contract simply wouldn't be renewed, which might be the first time they heard about their need to improve.

Catmull says that keeping employees happy and making sure Pixar, and later Disney Animation, were great places to work was the best way to ensure that their most talented people stayed with them. Catmull believes that it's much better to deal with problems quickly than to ignore them because there's a contract in place. He says people realize they won't always get what they want but that knowing they will be genuinely heard is important.

Another interesting perspective on agreements comes from John Paul Lederach, a peace negotiator who works in war zones and the author of *The Moral Imagination: The Art and Soul of Building Peace*. The agreements he is talking about are peace agreements and truces:

What is the agreement? It is of course the signed document. But even the person in the street in settings of armed conflict will say, "No, it is not the paper." So, beyond the paper, what is the agreement? I find time and again that the prevailing image of agreement is the notion of solution… Agreement creates the expectation that the conflict has ended. This assumes of course that the agreement represents substantive solutions to specific problems and that we can in some way characterize the agreement as solutions that are to be sustained…

However, in the end, if we accept this view, we pay a price… People are led to believe that the key to changing the situation lies in some kind of miraculous solution. Intuitively, they do not believe the signed paper will make that much difference. And their intuition is correct. Signed papers do not make a difference, and the agreements collapse unless the deeper processes of genuine engagement are created.

So are contracts relevant in long-term business relationships? The answer is yes but in a slightly different way than is normally considered. A contract is an archeological document, an excavation of problems that have arisen in the past, and each provision is based on a past conflict.

Reviewing this inventory of past problems acts as a business planning exercise. A contract review forces the parties to consider a number of scenarios and potential problems and to develop solutions. As Logica confirms, well-thought-out contract terms form an effective underpinning but not an effective enforcement tool. Long-term business relationships, like the one you'll form when you hire your buyer, require engagement, not enforcement.

The Science of Win-Win

If we accept that trust is important, we need to consider the type of relationship in which trust can grow. Because trust itself is not automatic. In fact as we all know, the automatic default is more likely to be not trusting. David DeSteno is a professor of psychology who has researched and written about trust. His studies have shown that most people will cheat if they believe they will not be caught and no one will be harmed.

DeSteno has tried to determine the situations in which trust is low and those in which trust is high. His studies confirm that trust is lowest in short-term relationships. This is because without something to be gained in the future there is no motivation to be trustworthy. Trust is also quite low in relationships where there is an imbalance of power and one person controls the other. Common sense, really, but the research confirms it.

The studies show that the highest likelihood for trust is in a long-term relationship in which neither party controls the other and both parties benefit. In other words, if we were to sit down to design a relationship that would have the highest likelihood of trust, we would design a win-win relationship, which is exactly the type of relationship that drives the hire your buyer philosophy.

Emotional Intelligence

Employee engagement, trust and win-win all seem to make sense, but for those of us stuck in an "I'm great" world, how do we make the switch? The answer lies in developing emotional intelligence.

It is hard to believe but the term "emotional intelligence" was not widely used until 1995, especially given that its counterpart, artificial intelligence, became widely known in 1956. In 1995 psychologist Daniel Goleman wrote the bestseller *Emotional Intelligence: Why It Can Matter More than IQ*. The term EQ is often used as a short form.

To illustrate the cost of a lack of EQ, Goleman writes about airline pilot Melburn McBroom. McBroom's temper was so bad that his copilots did not tell him that the plane was running out of fuel while McBroom tried to sort out a landing-gear problem. The plane crashed and 10 people died. Ironically it was McBroom's skill that saved most on the plane when he took the controls and skillfully avoided houses, trees and wires, belly-landing in an empty field. This incident is now a standard part of the behavioral aspect of professional pilot training to ensure it never happens again.

EQ is what separates Stage 3 from Stage 4 in business. To teach the lessons of EQ to businesspeople Goleman wrote an article for *Harvard Business Review* in 1998 called "What Makes a Leader?" *HBR* describes it as one of its top 10 "must-read" articles.

For the article Goleman researched 188 global companies. He found that the traditional leadership qualities – intellectual intelligence, strength, purpose and vision – are insufficient for success. He says, "We all know a story about someone extremely qualified who is promoted to a leadership role only to fail, while another person who does not stand out is promoted and succeeds brilliantly." The difference, he says, is that truly effective leaders have five EQ qualities: self-awareness, self-regulation, motivation, empathy and social skills.

These EQ qualities may sound "soft" and certainly not technical, but Goleman found direct ties between EQ and measurable business results. He points out that many leaders are hired for technical skills and fired for lack of EQ. Let's look at why these qualities are so important.

» **Self-Awareness:** Leaders have to know themselves and be able to push and expand their limits. A self-aware leader knows when to ask for help and takes calculated risks, which leads to confidence. An ability to laugh at oneself and use humor in a self-deprecating way is a sign of a leader with EQ.

» **Self-Regulation:** The ability to control yourself and your impulses creates consistency of behavior. You can suspend judgment and reconsider positions. This makes a leader predictable and reliable. People are comfortable and trusting because they know the probable outcome – at least from an emotional perspective – of an encounter with the boss.

» **Motivation:** Leaders with EQ want to achieve, grow and learn for the enjoyment of it. The lower emotions of greed and fear do not drive them. These traits lead to optimism and a higher energy level.

» **Empathy:** EQ is not about sympathy, it's about empathy. Empathy is a thoughtful consideration of employees' feelings – along with other factors – to make strategic choices about how to deal with and engage employees.

» **Social Skills:** A leader has to delegate to get other people to do work; social skills facilitate this. Leaders need to build consensus in groups and drive change. Goleman describes social skills as "friendliness with a purpose: moving people in the direction you desire." Those with high EQ can accomplish this without being manipulative, pushy or abusive.

These EQ qualities need to be developed to build an effective team. The other qualities we have discussed in this chapter – trust, building long-term business relationships and win-win – can also all be developed. We will look at these and other vital skills in the next chapter.

Chapter 5
The Martial Art of Win-Win: Mastering Soft Skills

The Way of Combining Forces

WE HAVE REVIEWED the lose-lose culture of litigation and the win-lose culture of Stage 3: "I'm great, you're not." We have considered the benefits of engagement, trust, win-win relationships, operating at a Stage 4 "We're great" level and emotional intelligence. This chapter discusses the skills necessary to combine those forces. The term "martial art" is used to convey the idea that this is not a naive pursuit. We do not trust because we are gullible, we trust because it creates value. Developing value-creating trust is a deep skill, like a martial art, that requires dedication and practice.

Aikido is a Japanese martial art; its name means the "way of combining forces." Like many martial arts aikido is defensive; there are no attacking moves in aikido. It is not necessary to be physically strong because the opponent's strength and force are used against them to redirect them away or to the ground. The central tenet of aikido is that the opponent not be injured.

On its website, California martial arts studio The Way writes

We do not train to fight; we train so we do not have to fight.

In martial arts, we learn to fight, so we can learn to interact. Fighting is very elemental – it has to do with survival. To learn to interact with peace, intention, and control at an elemental level allows us to bring these same qualities to *all* our interactions. Through the medium of martial arts, we learn self-mastery.

Students are expected to strive to their personal best both in martial arts training and in other aspects of life. They are expected to compete only against themselves and their own limitations and to show respect for their fellow students and other human beings at all times. The emphasis is on tolerance and respect for other ways and ideas and on always seeking a non-violent resolution to conflict.

Martial arts are about mastery of the emotions and about interacting defensively, respectfully and without harm. The message is, "We could have hurt each other, but isn't it better to interact this way?"

TO MOVE TO STAGE 4
MASTER THE SOFT SKILLS

STAGE 4
WE'RE GREAT!

PROFESSIONAL   EXPERT AT WORK   HIRE YOUR BUYER

STAGE 3
I'M GREAT! YOU'RE NOT

Win-win is not a naive pursuit. It is important to restate that you can get to Stage 4, "We're great," only by traveling through Stage 3, "I'm great." Win-win is the game you play after you have become great, not before. Win-win is a gathering of masters for the benefit of all.

Where do you start? Some people maintain that it's impossible to be truthful, accountable, aware and collaborative unless you are in a safe environment. They feel it is too dangerous to always tell the truth and to boldly take responsibility for their actions. The irony is that it's precisely these behaviors that create safe environments. The more individuals tell the truth, are accountable for the consequences of their choices, strive to increase self-awareness and communicate their good intentions, the greater the chances for successful collaboration. Think about that in the context of your business.

To navigate safely and effectively in the world of win-win you need greater skills, not lesser ones. You need a way of combining forces. You have to be deliberate and strategic in the manner in which you interact with the world. Like a martial art, win-win is based on forces that can be more skillfully handled with practice and application.

The Forces of Win-Win

The forces of win-win are people skills – "soft skills." Most business owners focus on the hard technical issues. Like Google's engineers writing and debugging code, hard issues are measurable and provable. For most people it's easier to deal with the hard technical aspects of the job. "Hard" implies that something is more worthwhile than something "soft." People like to describe themselves as hardworking; whoever heard of someone going to the gym to get soft or wanting to be soft-headed?

But modern management theory holds that soft skills drive hard numbers. A survey of 1,200 international executives by Bain & Company found that nine out of 10 executives place equal value on corporate culture and corporate strategy. Corporate culture is the collective values, beliefs and emotions displayed by the employees and owners of a business. Culture is the way in which people interact and treat one another. Culture is a soft issue.

Every business has a culture. The question is whether it is a stagnant culture or a vibrant one that creates value. The answer lies in your ability to combine the forces of win-win.

When I speak of these forces I do so with a humility hardened through 25 years of watching the emotional wreckage of the litigation system – a system based on a lack of trust.

*Inter*dependence

Three of Stephen R. Covey's *7 Habits of Highly Effective People* deal with creating interdependence. Covey believed that to be highly effective, an individual must move beyond independence and become interdependent. The three interdependence habits Covey prescribed are to think win-win, to seek first to understand and to synergize.

Win-win seeks mutual benefit in all human interactions. Covey said,

> Most of us learn to base our self-worth on comparisons and competition. We think about succeeding in terms of someone else failing – that is, if I win, you lose; or if you win, I lose. Life becomes a zero-sum game.

> Win-win sees life as a cooperative arena, not a competitive one. Win-win is a frame of mind and heart that constantly seeks mutual benefit in all human interactions. Win-win means agreements or solutions are mutually beneficial and satisfying.

. . . .

To navigate safely and effectively in the world of win-win you need greater skills, not lesser ones. You need a way of combining forces.

. . . .

The next Covey habit for interdependence is "seek first to understand." This habit involves empathic listening, which is listening both to the rational, verbal part of the communication and to the emotion the person is feeling. Empathetic listening is active and includes seeing the person, their body language and expression, their nuance and their pain.

Understanding the emotion a person is feeling allows you to create a deeper sense of trust in the relationship. This type of listening allows the other person to listen to you. Reciprocal empathetic listening allows for the highest degree of problem exploration and resolution. Business owners can use this habit in every relationship they have.

The last Covey habit dealing with interdependence is to synergize. Synergize means to create more than the sum of the individual inputs. Strengths are combined through positive teamwork to achieve goals no one person could have alone. Abraham Maslow described synergy as a natural outcome when self-actualizing people work together. Synergy is a core driver of value in business succession.

Synergy pours out of a Stage 4 "We're great" environment. This is a description of a "we're great" environment from *Tribal Leadership*:

> Teams are the norm, focused around shared values and a common purpose. Information moves freely throughout the group. People's relationships are built on shared values. They tend to ask, "what's the next right thing to do?" and to build ad hoc partnerships to accomplish what's important at the moment. Their language focuses on "we," not "me." If two people get in a squabble, a third will step in and repair the relationship rather than create a personal following for himself. Unlike Stage Two, the group is composed of people who have played the Stage Three game and won – and are ready for genuine partnerships.

That's the rational explanation. To build "we're great" you need to foster a more emotionally intelligent connection – trust, reciprocation, loyalty – with your team.

Quality Is Not an Add-On

The creation of quality is an interesting skill. It is the physical manifestation of trust. When you look admiringly at a car and talk about its quality craftsmanship, what you really mean is that the car is trustworthy – what it promises to do, it will do, and it will keep doing it.

W. Edwards Deming was a technical wizard who revolutionized manufacturing methods by infusing the entire process with quality. His internship at Bell Laboratories was in statistical modeling and process control. His PhD, from Yale, was in mathematics and physics. Quality is measured statistically in terms of defect rates per million and overall consistency. But statistics do not produce quality, they just measure it.

Deming discovered that quality was not something you could add on at the end of the line. In a famous example Ford workers used rubber mallets to tap doors into the proper place after the car rolled off the assembly line so that they would close properly. Ford executives were surprised to learn that Toyota had no rubber mallets at the end of the line. There was no need: the doors, hinges, posts and frames were all built properly from the beginning. Quality needs to be an integral part of each step in the process.

So how do you achieve quality?

Deming developed the 14 principles of quality management published in his 1982 book *Out of the Crisis*. These principles form the basis of the modern quality and lean manufacturing movements. Read the six Deming principles set out below and ask yourself which ones relate to statistical skills and which to soft skills:

» Adopt the new philosophy. We are in a new economic age. Western management must awaken to the challenge, learn its responsibilities and take on leadership for change.
» Stop depending on inspection (control) to achieve quality. Eliminate the need for inspection by building quality into the product in the first place.
» Move toward having a single supplier for any one item. Develop a long-term relationship built on loyalty and trust.
» Continuously improve the system of production and service to improve quality and productivity and thus constantly decrease costs.
» Institute training on the job, along with a vigorous program of education and self-improvement.
» Drive out fear, so that everyone may work effectively for the company.

Hearing Emotions:
The Sound of Flowers Opening

An important EQ skill is knowing how to hear emotions.

To learn how to hear emotions you have to visualize the person you are communicating with as two people. One of them is the rational and legalistic person you normally communicate with; the other is the emotional person you normally ignore. Listen very carefully and replay the conversation a second time to hear the emotional content of the message. All your senses can help you see beyond the words to the emotions running across the person's face.

Hearing emotions is surprisingly easy. We are all emotional creatures, but we have learned to suppress emotions, pretending we don't have them. If we just let ourselves be calm, the emotions will bubble up and we'll be able to feel them in ourselves and in others.

Crafting communication so that it addresses both the rational and the emotional person is much more effective and efficient than targeting only the rational being. In a group, it is quite empowering when you can craft messages that address everyone's fears. This dual approach also leads to much more client-centric planning – the type of planning that facilitates success.

A Zen fable makes the point about hearing emotions.

A young prince is sent to study under a great Chinese master. The master says that to be a great ruler the prince must learn to hear the unheard. The master says the prince must spend a month in the forest alone, away from the noise of the palace and then return to describe what he has heard.

When the prince returns, he reports that he has heard bluebirds singing and branches breaking and falling, the flapping wings of hawks, the cicadas, the wind in the trees and the rush of the stream. The master says these are sounds anyone can hear. An emperor must hear more. The prince returns to the forest, but he is unsure what the master meant.

One day he tries to hear among the other sounds something he has not heard before. When he returns, he tells the master, "When I tried to find new sounds I had to listen for what I had not heard before. Then I could hear the unheard – the sound of flowers opening, the sun warming the earth and the grass drinking the morning dew." The master nods. "A great ruler must hear the unheard. A great ruler must listen closely to the people's hearts, to their uncommunicated feelings, unexpressed pain and unspoken complaints. Only then can he hope to inspire confidence, understand when something is wrong, and truly meet his people's needs."

The Value of Intuition

Intuition is understanding without the intermediary of reasoning. No one can explain how we are able to reason, so why is intuition any less valid a way of coming to understanding?

David DeSteno, the professor of psychology whose research on trust we reviewed in the last chapter, talks about the value of intuition in determining trust. He says that too often people disregard their intuition or gut feelings in favor of rational analysis; he views this as a mistake:

> Our minds come with built-in trust detectors. [Research results] also reinforce how valuable intuitions, or gut feelings, can be. The problem is that managers and negotiators often suppress their intuitive machinery by either (a) ignoring it in favor of what they believe to be more rational predictors for trustworthiness, such as reputation or status, or (b) mistakenly looking for the wrong nonverbal "tells."

> I suggest allowing your mind to arrive undisturbed at a judgment. Recent research led by Marc-André Reinhard of the University of Mannheim confirms the efficacy of this approach. The researchers had participants watch videos of honest and deceptive people. Immediately afterward, half the participants were encouraged to deliberate on who was trustworthy, while the others were told to distract themselves with a different task. The latter group proved to be significantly more accurate in subsequently identifying who was trustworthy. Why? Distraction allowed their non-conscious minds to extract meaning from the multitude of nonverbal cues unimpeded by analytical interference.

A highly renowned Ontario Court of Appeal judge once described trusting intuition as the "tummy test," meaning that he usually decided a case on the basis of whether it felt right. Most often the lawyers appearing before him, on both sides, agreed with his decisions. This is an example of a highly developed sense of trust in your own intuition, a skill that is tied to and guided by your emotions.

Questions: Pulling the Explanations Out

Questions are another essential skill of win-win and they are a tool you can easily learn to use in your business to build trust and empathy among your team. Tom Deans has written two books, *Every Family's Business: 12 Common Sense Questions to Protect Your Wealth* and *Willing Wisdom: 7 Questions Successful Families Ask*. Each book takes a deep dive into a complex and difficult area of the family relationship. The first is parents and children in the family business. The second is death and legacy in the family.

These areas are emotion-filled and communicating about them is often considered taboo. Lack of communication leads to unnecessary misunderstanding, pain and damaged or destroyed relationships.

Empathic listening is the key to understanding. But to listen the other person has to speak and explain. Questions are the hooks that pull the explanations out.

Effective questions are the basis of medical diagnosis and court room cross-examination. Einstein said 90% of scientific effort should be directed at developing the right question. Listening occurs only during responses and the better the quality of the questions, the better the quality of the responses. With enough time and the right questions you could understand everything that reasoning and intuition can comprehend.

The basis of each of Deans's books is a set of questions designed to puncture family taboos. He says, "Silence is the great destroyer of wealth; these questions get the family talking." The primary lesson for me is that questions can be used to create culture. In *Willing Wisdom* Deans writes that culture means relationships and that relationships are "formed through talking."

A relationship is the way in which two or more people are connected, or the state of being connected. Our personal culture is formed by those to whom we are connected and by the quality of those connections.

Effective business succession is to a large extent about the owner creating a new and improved culture with family, advisors, employees, managers, successors and themselves. This means improving the connections the owner has with each of the groups in his or her life.

The seven questions in *Willing Wisdom* are designed to eliminate confusion, surprise and conflict at the most vulnerable of times – a death in the family. This book shines important light on this difficult situation and helps transform it into a meaningful and much less painful event for the family. Deans notes that 60% of North Americans do not even have a will. Instead of fearing death people should be speaking openly about it. Parents should let their children know the terms of the will and those terms should be discussed and agreed to by the rest of the family.

. . . .

Effective business succession is to a large extent about the owner creating a new and improved culture with family, advisors, employees, managers, successors and themselves.

. . . .

Every Family's Business has 12 questions. William Cartwright, the book's fictional son who worked with his father to sell the family business, says he and his father would go through the 12 questions every year. The questions expose most of the common problem areas family businesses face. The questions can be adapted for an owner and an employee who is buying into the business. Here are a few of the questions:

» What does our family business look like in five years?
» Are you interested in buying stock and acquiring control?
» I agree that within the next 60 days I will put in place a special compensation formula for my child in the event the business is sold in the next five years. Yes or no.
» SWOT analysis. List the top three strengths, weaknesses, opportunities and threats that could affect the business over the next five years. Then compare, discuss and develop consensus.
» I agree to conduct an annual performance review of my child. This review will measure performance against mutually agreed-on and achievable goals and objectives. New goals and objectives will be set for the coming year. Yes or no.

I particularly like the last one. When it comes to business, owners should view their children objectively, as if they were any other employee. If the children have the desire and skills or aptitude they get the job. If not, they should be allowed to self-actualize elsewhere and supported in their pursuits.

The real point is not the questions themselves, but the fact that questions and empathic listening are the tools that build a healthy culture. You could use some, none or all of Deans's questions as long as you use questions that pull explanations out and eliminate confusion and uncertainty.

Deans's questions seem quite straightforward, like Google's top manager qualities, but this belies their power. As simple as they seem it is hard to see how there could be confusion or anxiety about unexpressed intentions if you and your family or key employees fully discuss the questions each year.

The Force of Trust

Trust is the most important force that's part of win-win; it is therefore important to develop a deeper, more specific meaning of trust. Consider these observations on trust:

> » The force of trust runs in both directions. It is important to be trustworthy and it is important to understand who else is trustworthy.
> » Trust pays a dividend in long-term business relationships that require flexibility, compromise and growth.
> » In developing the force of trust it is very useful to rely on your own intuition or emotional reactions.
> » If there is low or no trust do not enter a long-term business relationship.
> » If the scope of the transaction can be quantified and controlled, trust may not be necessary.
> » View trust as a hard skill; its value can be quantified.
> » Contract terms and penalties are insufficient governance tools. They work best with one-off, short-term relationships.
> » In long-term business relationships contracts are useful as a planning exercise for defining the scope of responsibilities and expectations. Trust, however, is a far better mechanism for filling in missing or ambiguous understanding than is judicial interpretation.

In *The Great Workplace: How to Build It, How to Keep It, and Why It Matters* authors Michael Burchell and Jennifer Robin note that trust is the single most important quality:

> We often joke that our jobs as consultants would be so much easier if we could help leaders roll out a "Trust Policy." Essentially, it would decree that from this day forward, everyone will trust everyone else. In some ways, building trust is easier than generating a policy; all it requires you to do is to behave differently. In other ways, though, building trust is infinitely more difficult. It requires you to consider the impacts of your decisions on relationships, to craft and support organizational policies and procedures that position your managers to do the same, and to build a self-sustaining system of trust with the employees.

Control: The Force Standing in the Way of Win-Win

We have looked at many of the forces of win-win but it is also necessary to look at the force standing in the way of win-win: that force is *control*. Because of the complexity of explaining the problem of control and how and when to give it up, we will spend the rest of this chapter looking at it.

Control is a central paradox of business succession. On one hand, control is essential and no one wants to give up control because they will be vulnerable and unsafe. On the other hand, giving up control is the inevitable result of business succession. If you do not give up control in an orderly way it will be lost through an emergency.

Control has many definitions and aspects. Consider that business itself is a highly controlled activity. Products meet specifications. Customers have expectations; you can't hand over forks when someone asks for pants. Banks expect payments, laws have to be followed. All societal forces exert powerful controls on the types of freedoms we have. Everyone knows we must maintain self-control. The opposite of control is chaos, where nothing gets done. The question, then, is how much control do we need?

If we were to take control to its extreme we would double up: we would have someone sit beside each employee and whisper instructions in their ear moment to moment. Doing this would require a duplicate set of employees who control the employees actually doing the work. This is the doubling up problem. It is not as far-fetched as it seems; indeed, entire societies have operated this way for millennia.

Dictatorships have very large armies. It was not uncommon in some dictatorships to have 50% (or more) of the population in the military; they controlled the other 50%, who were working to support the military. In Nazi Germany 100% of the population was either in the military or working to support the military; children were expected to report parents who were not completely loyal to the Aryan code. This type of society is an extreme example of the power-based relationships that Logica described as not being very effective.

This same problem occurs to a lesser extent in a bureaucracy and is expressed through excessive rules and red tape. To the eyes of an entrepreneur it seems that a bureaucracy has many redundant non-productive employees – but the entrepreneur misses the point. The purpose of these redundant non-productive employees is to "spy" on the other employees and ensure that the myriad rules and regulations, which often conflict, are followed to the letter.

The Battle Paradox

Another control problem is the battle paradox. The purpose of the military is to be prepared for battle. The battle paradox is that plans for battle are useful until the battle starts and then the battle itself directs the plan. Military personnel have to understand how to fight without a plan – to fight in chaos. Armies that are excessively controlled are much less efficient and much less successful. Excessive control actually puts you in peril.

Sports are a civilized form of battle. Basketball coach Phil Jackson has a sophisticated coaching philosophy. He studied Zen, Eastern mysticism and the ways of the Lakota Indians. He did not believe in controlling his players or coaching from the sidelines. It is important to note that Jackson distinguished between *control* and *final authority*. Occasionally someone has to use final authority to break a tie vote, but it is a power to be used rarely. Jackson wanted his players to have freedom, responsibility and creativity in the way they played. He says,

After years of experimenting, I discovered that the more I tried to exert power directly, the less powerful I became. I learned to dial back my ego and distribute power as widely as possible without surrendering final authority. Paradoxically, this approach strengthened my effectiveness because it freed me to focus on my job as keeper of the team's vision. Some coaches insist on having the last word, but I always tried to foster an environment in which everyone played a leadership role, from the most un-schooled rookie to the veteran superstar. If your primary objective is to bring the team into a state of harmony and oneness, it doesn't make sense for you to rigidly impose your authority.

Jackson saw a number of weaknesses in the controlling coaching method. The controlling coach has to coach from the sidelines, first deciding the play and then calling it; the players have to hear it and then finally play it. This four-part hesitation creates opportunity for opponents who are paying attention and do not need to wait for instruction.

Jackson developed a more difficult style of game that allowed play in the moment. This method provided players with the opportunity to develop their own leadership styles without hesitation or prediction. Jackson's teams were dynamic and surprisingly difficult to read. They captured many opportunities while giving up few. Jackson was giving freedom and harnessing responsibility.

Entrepreneurs know that rigid rules don't work so they abandon rules and govern through instinct. Ironically many entrepreneurs don't allow their employees the same latitude because they don't believe the employees are capable of working effectively without direction – "I'm great, you're not."

Freedom and Responsibility

The control we are concerned about is the control that prevents growth, creativity and self-actualization. It is the control exerted in a power-based relationship. This problematic control manifests as micromanagement and lack of delegation. Control imposed by contract terms, penalties and orders is a form of control that soothes the insecure but produces inferior results – the trust tax instead of the trust dividend. This type of control creates value quicksand.

The solution is to give employees freedom, but not a freedom that creates chaos. Yin and yang are opposites that depend on each other like shadow and sunlight. If freedom is the yin, responsibility is the yang. In his book *Good to Great: Why Some Companies Make the Leap... and Others Don't,* Jim Collins describes it this way: "The good-to-great companies built a consistent system with clear constraints, but they also gave people freedom and responsibility within the framework of that system. They hired self-disciplined people who didn't need to be managed, and then managed the system, not the people."

The yin-yang of freedom and responsibility exerts a natural control, much like a forest that is free to grow but at the same time reflects balance and symmetry.

Natural control is not an add-on. Like quality, natural control does not come from rules or quotas. Natural control emanates from a deep, trusting place of purpose and engagement where people are freed – not afraid – to achieve.

We have reviewed control in the workplace, so let's head on up to the big one: legal control.

Legal Control

Give up my votes? Are you nuts?

Most trusted advisors tell you never to give up legal control. Legal control usually comes from the number of voting shares you own. If you have more than 50% of the voting shares you have control of the business. With control you can make all the important decisions: hiring the CEO, voting for directors, selling the business.

Phil Jackson talked about being the final authority on the team. Legal control gives you this final authority. About the use of final authority Jackson says, "Rules reduce freedom and responsibility. Enforcement of rules is coercive and manipulative, which diminishes spontaneity and absorbs group energy. The more coercive you are, the more resistant the group will become. Leaders should practice becoming more open. The wise leader is of service: receptive, yielding, following."

The force of legal control should not be used in win-win situations except to conduct legal formalities. Legal control is to be quarantined so that it cannot be used against you. When used at all it is to be used defensively in ways that harm no one.

A very common voting control problem involves parents who don't want to let go. When the parent is simply being selfish it is a disservice to the children, who cannot fully mature if they cannot participate in control. The problem is much worse if the parent does not trust the children with control. By delaying the transfer of control the parent is creating a problem that is only fully realized on the death or disability of the parent, when they can no longer help. If the children genuinely cannot control the business it should be sold.

I suggest that owners look at control in three phases.

In the first phase the owner retains final authority but actively encourages the employee team to start making decisions. In this phase owners restrain themselves from exercising final authority. When the owner does that, employees learn to make decisions on their own. If you find it necessary to resort to your final authority because the employees' decisions are wrong or you just don't like them, that's probably a sign that hiring your buyer won't work for you. If, however, you can go for a few years without exercising final authority, you are probably ready for Phase 2.

In Phase 2 the owner gives up final authority and enters a true partnership in which everyone has an equal voice. If that works well for a few years, the owner can consider Phase 3.

In Phase 3 the owner gives up all votes and becomes an advisor. This may take 20 years to accomplish but giving up control completely is the ultimate goal.

We have seen that employee engagement and trust both create value. What about giving up control – would that create value? Let's have a look.

Does Giving Up Control Create Value?

Let's knock off the easy one first. We know that giving up operational control creates value because we know that delegation equals value. The less the business depends on the owner for decisions, the more transferable value it has.

Could it be the same with legal control?

Research on tech start-ups confirms that the founder has a choice – to remain in control or create value. Harvard business professor Noam Wasserman's research directly links founder control to start-up value:

Startups in which the founder is still in control of the board of directors and/or the CEO position are significantly less valuable than those in which the founder has given up a degree of control. More specifically, on average, each additional degree of founder control reduces the value of the startup by 23.0%–58.1%.

Consider the traditional advice given to entrepreneurs: "make sure you keep 51% of the shares." If this is the best advice, one would expect that the best entrepreneurs, people like Bill Gates, would have followed it. Did he?

Not only did Bill Gates not have 51% of Microsoft's shares, he had only 15%. But this 15% was enough to make him the world's richest man for many years, despite the fact that he gives a lot of his wealth away.

Here's something to consider: had Bill Gates followed traditional advice about voting control, we may never have heard of him.

Noam Wasserman surveyed 6,130 US start-ups in the tech and life sciences industries. The results were consistent across industries. Wasserman provides a simple compelling reason why it makes sense to give up some control:

> At the beginning of the founding journey, the vast majority of entrepreneurs are missing key resources, in the form of financial capital, human capital, and/or social capital. By attracting those resources to the company, founders have a better chance of growing a more valuable company. For instance, by attracting cofounders, hires, or investors, founders can access skills, contacts, and money they were lacking.

. . . .

Had Bill Gates followed traditional advice about voting control, we may never have heard of him.

. . . .

A succession journey is very similar to a founding journey. The difference is that the entrepreneur has already built a solid foundation for the business. The start-up aspect of succession is building the second and third floors of value on top of the foundation. The owner needs to hire a buyer to take on the labor aspects of this buildup. This requires the owner, over time, to give up control to create value – a choice very similar to the one Bill Gates made.

In a situation where you have to have a staged transfer of control, the forces of trust and win-win become critically important. If you have properly developed the forces of trust and win-win you are in the zone that offers the highest probability of protection from the abuse of control after it's transferred. If you have picked and trained the team properly you have the highest chance of the business being sustained long enough to pay you out in full and continuing to be a business that you can be proud you created.

In the next chapter we examine the pulleys and levers of value creation.

Chapter 6

Value Creation: Strategic Growth

"Of Course I Create Value!"

MOST LIFESTYLE BUSINESS OWNERS have created a good job for themselves. Larry Summers, past president of Harvard University, said, "At Harvard we don't teach you how to get a job, we teach you how to create one." So most lifestyle business owners walk in good company. The difficulty arises when the owner realizes that other people will not pay a lot of money to buy someone's job and certainly not enough to sustain a decent lifestyle in the third stage of life.

The problem is that most owners are not creating transferable value. If you ask most owners whether they create value they would probably respond, "Of course what I do has value for my clients." And that answer is true. But it misses the fact that most are not creating value *in their business*.

Robert T. Slee wrote a very interesting valuation textbook called *Private Capital Markets*. He makes the astute observation that almost all MBA finance courses focus on teaching finance theory that applies to public companies. Prior to Slee's text there was no comprehensive theory for valuing private businesses. This is because *private* company information is confidential, unlike *public* company information. Slee's ambitious book examines public company valuation theory and translates it into a conceptual framework that applies to private companies.

As Slee explains, one factor that creates a lot of value for a public company is that they can print money by issuing shares. Facebook did this when it bought WhatsApp for $19 billion. Facebook paid $4 billion in cash and $15 billion in shares and options. Facebook didn't have to go to the bank and apply for a loan or use a credit card. All they had to do was call their lawyer and ask, "If you have some time after lunch, can you print up $15 billion for us?" This ability to print money, referred to as "low-cost financing," is a major reason that public companies trade at higher multiples than private companies.

When private companies print shares there is a real cost. The TV show *Shark Tank* often features heated discussions about the value of the shares and whether the investor should get 30% or 50% of the company. On *Shark Tank* you can't just print it.

Pepperdine University, in consultation with Rob Slee, started the Private Capital Markets Project. The purpose of the PCM Project is to "advance ongoing research to understand the true cost of private capital across market types and the investment expectations of privately held business owners." Apparently watching *Shark Tank* a few times isn't enough.

Slee has a very simple formula for determining whether value is being created in a business: does the return on investment exceed the cost of capital? If so, you are creating value. If not, you are destroying value. Looking at a survey for the PCM Project, Slee found that about 80% of business owners were in fact *not* creating value, despite working hard and taking great risk. Why? Slee says,

> The goal of most owners is for the business to generate a good lifestyle for themselves and their families. It's hard to blame them for this, as these same owners have no value creation conceptual framework from which to leverage. Owners seem to think that you can't have both a valuable business and a great lifestyle. So they choose the nearest path... which is to drain the business while they can.

> For several decades this strategy somewhat worked, because owners could yank money out of the business and invest in real estate and securities. While the business was not valuable, the owners had outside assets that were. I've personally seen hundreds of situations where – since the business has no value – an owner does a walk-away when it's time to retire.

So why aren't most owners trying to create more valuable businesses now? 90%+ of the owners have no idea what it takes to create a highly valuable business.

The problem is compounded by the fact that many owners misunderstand the term "cost of capital." They assume that cost of capital relates to debt. But the capital Slee is talking about is the amount of money tied up in your business. Under this definition capital means the value of the business. Whatever your business is worth is your investment in that business. The cost of capital is the opportunity cost of investing that value somewhere else. You should ask yourself this: if I could sell my business, would I be better off investing in another opportunity?

What Return Do You Expect from Your Investment?

You should be looking at both aspects of your business: the job side of it and the investment aspect. If the value of your business is not growing, you are not getting a return on the money (value) tied up in it. All you really have is a job, not an investment. Worse yet, most of your net worth is tied up in a very risky asset that is not paying a return.

. . . .

About 80% of business owners were in fact
not creating value.

. . . .

How risky? Consider the return that the sharks are looking for when they invest in risky private companies. According to the PCM Project, venture capital investors want a 45% annual return. Even if you are the one in 100 they would invest in, they want half your company and they expect it to double in value in three years.

And what return do most owners expect? Rob Slee says none. Really?

Setting aside lifestyle considerations, from a purely financial perspective, most owners would be better off to sell the business, invest the money and get a job somewhere else.

Business Valuation Is Not about Value, It's an Audit of Risk

One of the entrepreneurial paradoxes is that opportunities emerge out of risk – no risk, no opportunity. But valuators cannot see opportunity. Risk is the reason that valuators discount the range of multiples to between 3× and 6×. Business valuators do not consider the opportunity or potential of the business, they measure the risks to determine the probability that the free cash flow will continue in the future.

Risks are real. After a farmer plants, the seeds should grow. But there could be flood, fire or pestilence. A good friend told me that his crops failed two years in a row. In the third year, two days before harvest, he watched a hailstorm destroy his 400-acre crop in 20 minutes. Sadly, bankruptcy was the only option.

More than 50% of mergers do not return their cost of capital. Acquisition failure is a real risk. Valuators have to keep a multitude of risks in mind and they have a professional obligation to be conservative. Conservatism is a good thing when it protects you from risk.

Entrepreneurs Are Not Gamblers

Consider the Dictionary.com definition of entrepreneur: "a person who organizes and manages any enterprise, especially a business, usually with considerable initiative and risk." In other words, an entrepreneur looks at risk from the opposite side of the spectrum. If an entrepreneur had spoken to a valuator about the risks of starting the business, the valuator probably would have advised the entrepreneur not to do it because over time 80% of small businesses fail.

Entrepreneurs are not gamblers. They do not rely on blind luck, the toss of a coin or the pull of a slot. Entrepreneurs look realistically at a problem and say, "I understand the risks but I am confident that I have the skills to overcome them." This is not gambling, this is an example of what Roger Martin, dean of the Rotman School of Management, calls Integrative Thinking, which is a method of resolving paradox.

At the end of logic lies paradox. A simple example is the liar's paradox: "I always lie." Logic concludes that this statement must be both true and untrue at the same time. But logically something cannot be true and untrue at the same time. This is the scene where the android gets stuck in a logic loop, its eyes flash, circuits fuse and smoke drifts out of its ears as it slumps over. Logic cannot take us past paradox.

There are many paradoxes in business:

» The entrepreneur's opportunity lies in risk. Risk reduces value – therefore opportunity reduces value.
» A business must reduce costs and increase value.
» Change will destroy every business that exists today; therefore, every business must change.

The list goes on.

The answer to paradox is explained by Martin's theory of Integrative Thinking. Integrative Thinking is a more complex form of thinking; it is an applied form of philosophy. It sees the paradoxes and conflicting variables in all their dimensions. It processes all of that and integrates it into a solution. Martin says great leaders have this ability and it is this ability that allows them to sustain success over time.

Fortunately, Martin believes that Integrative Thinking can be practiced and learned. The first step is to embrace paradox rather than avoid it. The grand whammy of paradox is that within paradox lies opportunity.

This concept is reflected in Dan Sullivan's idea that "all of the things that oppose your goals are actually the raw material for achieving them." Sullivan's idea, which is fleshed out in his concept of the Strategy Circle, is that you need a strategy to overcome each thing that opposes your goal. The collective strategies built from the raw material of opposition are what provide the opportunity to achieve your goals.

Once a paradox is resolved or opposition overcome, we can look back and see that it was not a paradox at all. It was an incomplete picture; we could see a conflict, or opposition, but we did not yet see beyond it. Extending your vision beyond the kaleidoscope of opposition allows you to step past the point where everyone else stops. This is the opportunity of opposition.

The professions of law, valuation and accounting are all about proof and certainty. Accountants have a professional obligation to be conservative and avoid risk. These professions are not integrative. They don't accept risk and reconcile it, they reject risk and avoid it. They stop at the point of opposition or paradox.

Owners have to keep this in mind when they read valuations. A business valuation has no vision, it is simply a snapshot of a point in time. Business valuations are constrained by the limiting assumptions of that moment; they have to be based on objective evidence that exists at that moment. Opposition or paradox at that point in time can have a drastic effect on a valuation.

What may seem obvious to the entrepreneur is almost irrelevant in the valuation exercise. A valuation cannot look to the future except in a very limited way, and then only based on past results. A valuator, unlike an entrepreneur, cannot use opposition as raw material for achievement. A valuator measures the risks posed by opposition and then assumes they probably will not be overcome.

The Bullet Paradox: Stopping the Motion

Point-in-time thinking gives rise to the "bullet paradox." How do you see a moving bullet? You can photograph it. To take the picture you will need a projectile sensor, an extremely short-duration flash and a dark-room. With a little luck and good timing you can get a perfect picture of the bullet.

The problem is that in the picture the bullet is not moving. Bullets never move in pictures; you will never see a moving bullet. This is the bullet paradox. Movement does not occur in points of time. Similarly, businesses do not move in points of time, nor do they move in valuations. They are frozen.

The only person who can really see the motion of your business is you, the owner. The ability to see the motion that's invisible to everyone else means the owner doesn't have the same set of risks as a buyer. You have already proven you can manage the business. This means that the 50% or 70% failure rate of mergers is not your starting point. You know the business, you don't need to rely on incomplete due diligence. You do not have a professional obligation to be conservative. You are not constrained to the present moment. You can embrace paradox and opposition, mitigate the risks and solve the problems. In short, you can sustain the business and create value that is invisible and unreachable for everyone else.

Bringing Value into Existence

When Rob Slee talks about return on investment he is talking about growth in the value of the business. He says, "Value creation starts with strategic thinking and action."

We will talk about strategic thinking later. First we have to understand what "create" means. Create means to bring something into existence. So *creating* value means bringing value into existence.

Value is a form of magic. You cannot create value by itself. Value has no separate existence. You cannot go to the hardware store and buy the supplies to build value.

You can build a tree fort but you can't climb up to the fort, unpack the value and put it on a shelf. The value of a tree fort is that you and your friends can go up there with air guns and protect the backyard from monsters.

· · · · · · · · · · · · · ·

Growth and value are always there, waiting patiently for someone to bring them into existence.

· · · · · · · · · · · · · ·

Bringing is the action. When we act skillfully in accordance with strategic thinking, we bring value into existence. Where do we bring value from? No one knows. Value is a natural inherent quality. Looking out the window in springtime, value is all around you. The sun is the ultimate creator of value.

Value has a lot in common with growth. Growth is another form of magic. No one has the power to make something grow. But if you have the right supplies – seeds, earth, water and sunlight – and you combine them skillfully, you can bring growth into existence. Bringing growth or value into existence is like building the tree fort. Growth and value are always there, waiting patiently for someone to bring them into existence.

The Value Creation Formula

To get on with the "bringing" as it applies to value, it is helpful to understand the elements of value creation. You will recall from Chapter 2 that the business value formula has two elements, free cash flow and a multiple. These two elements provide a measure of value at a point in time. To create value, to bring it into existence, we need the third element: strategic growth. The value creation formula starts with the business value formula, free cash flow × multiple, and then multiplies it by strategic growth. It looks like this:

3 ELEMENTS OF VALUE CREATION

FREE CASH FLOW **X** MULTIPLE **X** STRATEGIC GROWTH

Strategic growth is similar to strategic value. Strategic value is a buyer's perception of the value they can create by bringing two companies together. The limitation is that strategic value is only a picture arising at a point in time. It does not capture motion, it is not magic, it does not grow. Strategic value is simply a measurement.

Rob Slee tells us to "increase the value of your investment." The problem is that this simple statement doesn't tell us how to do it. The answer to increasing the value of your investment lies in the use of the three atomic elements of value creation: free cash flow, multiple and strategic growth. Using these three elements we can more precisely define an increase in value as increasing the free cash flow and multiple used in the valuation of your business through strategic growth.

Before we get started, note that you may need to review this formula with your accountant or a valuator to really understand and apply it to your own business. They may suggest a different way to bring value to your company and that's fine because there are many ways to do this. The only real issue is that you do it as completely and as accurately as possible.

The First Element: Free Cash Flow

If you have reviewed the book's Appendix, "Seven Steps for Determining Business Value," you will have learned that one way to determine free cash flow looks like this:

» Determine earnings.
» Determine EBITDA (earnings before interest, taxes, depreciation and amortization).
» Normalize EBITDA.

This is your annual free cash flow or earning power. A valuation will use an average of three to five years of free cash flow.

We have learned that free cash flow is different from profit. Keep these two critical points in mind when you think about free cash flow:

1. **There isn't necessarily a connection between sales and free cash flow.** Sales can go down, but if you were losing money on those sales free cash flow will go up. Sales can go up, but if it costs more to complete those sales than the earnings they generate, free cash flow goes down. Free cash flow is connected to earnings, not sales. The key to doubling the value of your business is not simply doubling the size of it.

2. **Not all expenses are the same.** Some costs are actually investments that increase value. UPS's routing technology is an example. UPS discovered that left turns have two drawbacks: it takes five times longer to turn left than it does to turn right, and there are four times more accidents on left turns than right turns. Left turns cost more time, gas and insurance. By spending money on GPS routing technology UPS eliminated 90% of left turns, which saved the company over 10 million gallons of fuel per year, plus the time wasted burning the gas, and it significantly reduced insurance costs. On UPS's financial statement this routing technology will appear as an expense but it is actually a very profitable investment.

You often hear owners say they want a one-year payback on an investment. This means that whatever they spend has to generate that amount in savings in the first year.

Let's look at that in valuation terms. If there is a one-year payback, the increase in value will be whatever you spent times whatever your multiple is. Let's say you spend $100,000 on design software that saves you $100,000 in design expenses in the first year. If you keep on saving this $100,000 each year, your annual free cash flow has increased by the $100,000 you saved. If your multiple is 5×, this $100,000 piece of design software increased your business value by $500,000. Spend as much as you can on investments that have a one-year payback and continue to generate that payback year after year.

Always know your free cash flow and set targets. Every year or every quarter, calculate your free cash flow so you can see whether you're on target.

The Second Element: Multiple

There is no magic to the term "multiple" – it simply comes from the word multiply. The magic is in how to get your multiple to multiply. The answer lies in managing risk.

A multiple is a reflection of risk. Risk refers to the fact that investors may lose their money. A guarantee means there is no risk of losing your money. A GIC is a *guaranteed* investment certificate. A GIC has no risk so the multiple is very high. A GIC that pays 2.5% per year has a multiple of 40 times (40×). That means that to get a return of $1.00 you need to invest $40 for a year; at a 40× multiple you have to invest 40 times as much money as you will be getting in return each year.

This may sound like a bad thing, but it isn't necessarily. Whether a 40× multiple is good or bad depends on risk. There are millions of people who want guaranteed no-risk investments even if the return is only 2.5%. For that kind of investor – let's say, a retiree – paying a 40× multiple is a good thing because there is no risk that they will lose their money.

At the other end of the scale is high risk. Let's look at the high-risk world of investing in a lifestyle business. We now reverse the numbers and say the investor wants a 40% return. An investment that pays 40% per year has a multiple of 2.5×. To get a return of $1.00 you need to invest $2.50 for a year. For that type of investor – let's say, the buyer of a business – paying a 2.5× multiple is a good thing because there is a lot of risk that they will lose their money.

But for the seller of the business, 2.5× is not so good. Unfortunately, many lifestyle businesses are at the 2.5× end of the scale and this is a bad thing if you can't afford to retire. If your free cash flow is $400,000 a year you have quite a decent living. But if the multiple is 2.5×, the business is worth only $1 million – not enough for you to be able to cash out and retire comfortably unless you have other investments.

John Warrillow, who developed the Sellability Score, describes in *Inc.* magazine how he came to understand the difference in multiples between large companies and small ones:

> Years ago I owned a little marketing and design agency and would rely on the multiples the big advertising agency holding companies got on the stock exchange to figure out its value. I'd assumed that, because Omnicom was trading at 22 times earnings, my little agency with $150,000 in profit was worth around $3 million.

> I got a wakeup call at an industry event when I found out that, in actuality, small ad agencies with less than $5 million in revenue were lucky to get three or four times pre-tax profit – much of which was tied to achieving goals in the future.

This doesn't sound so good, but if we use Integrative Thinking it leads to the most significant insight into the way you can grow your multiple. The starting point is to ask this question: why is it that a public company listed on a stock exchange has a multiple of 22× and a lifestyle business doing the same thing has a 3 or 4× multiple?

Actually, the better question is, why don't I get a 22× multiple, darn it!?

The answer is that risk grinds the multiple down. That's it – nothing else, just risk. Unfortunately, a lifestyle business has so many risks that the multiple can be ground down to one-tenth of the multiple of a public company in the same line of work.

But there is no need to tremble. All you have to do is reduce the risk, and like a child letting go of a birthday balloon, up goes your multiple.

The difference in multiples is one of the "big secrets" of the M&A business. Simply buying your business increases the value of a public company by several times what it paid you. Think about that for moment. Doing nothing at all increases the value of your business – sometimes by as much as 500% – but only *after* it is sold to a public company. The trick is the multiple. By doing nothing we know the free cash flow of your business doesn't change. But the multiple changes from your risky multiple to whatever multiple the public company has.

To illustrate this point, assume your company has a 5× multiple and the public company trades at 25×.

If your business is worth $1 million ($200,000 × your multiple of 5), then the day the public company buys it the value increases by 500% to $5 million ($200,000 × public company multiple of 25). This means that if you're selling your business it is very helpful to know the multiple of the purchaser – in other words, how much value can the buyer create in your company by doing nothing?

OK... So How Do I Double the Value?

A business with no processes, run on what's in the owner's head and based on personal goodwill, does not have much in the way of transferable value. To get the business out of your head you have to delegate to your employees. Doing less is more – delegation equals value. Delegation helps you get ready to sell, hire your buyer or otherwise transfer your business.

An example of working with multiples comes from Linas Jarasius, a founding partner of Swiss Avenue Partners, a firm that helps owners increase the value of their company. I saw him speak during Pinnacle Equity Solutions' Exit Planning Certification course in Boston (which, by the way, I highly recommend to advisors).

Jarasius asks a simple question: "How do you double the value of your business?" Most owners quickly answer, "Double the sales," but Jarasius said it is not easy to double sales quickly. For most owners, especially lifestyle business owners, it is much easier to double your multiple. You can double your multiple by delegating the business out of your head and into processes that others can follow without you being around.

Jarasius gave an example of quadrupling the value of your business. The example involves a five-year plan for a business with free cash flow of $400,000 and a multiple of 2.5×. That business is worth $1 million today. The first step is to double the multiple. If we develop a good business process and a good management team and convert personal goodwill to enterprise goodwill we should be able to double the multiple from 2.5× to 5×. This doubles the value of the business.

The second step is to double free cash flow. If free cash flow increases by 15% per year for five years, it doubles to $800,000. This means that in five years the value of the business has grown from $1 million ($400,000 × 2.5) to $4 million ($800,000 × 5). By doubling the multiple and doubling the free cash flow in five years, we quadruple the value of the business. Quadrupling the value of the business would solve a lot of problems for a lot of owners – and a lot of owners can do it.

Improving your business creates the double whammy effect: improving your business increases your free cash flow *and* increases your multiple.

Smith Furnishings was worth $12 million based on $3 million of free cash flow and a 4× multiple. Elizabeth Smith, the owner, hired a business process consultant to rework the manufacturing process. The consulting engagement cost $150,000 and Smith Furnishing saved $400,000 per year in expenses as a result of the new process, which improved the overall operations and prepared the company for expansion. Because the business improvement process addressed many weaknesses in the company, the company's multiple increased from 4× to 5×. Increasing the multiple from 4× to 5× resulted in a 25%, or $3 million, increase in the value of the company. The additional free cash flow of $400,000 at a 5× multiple added an additional $2 million to the company's value. So this $150,000 expenditure on process increased value by $5 million.

Another way to increase business value is to conduct an internal due diligence audit. Go through every item and question about your business that a hard-nosed M&A professional would go through. Fix everything you can. Find a valuation professional who will talk to you about risks in your business and what the likely increase to your multiple will be if you fix everything. Alternatively, use software such as the Value Opportunity Profile discussed in Chapter 2 to identify your value opportunity.

To appreciate the benefit of paying attention to the value formula, compare two hypothetical businesses with the same sales of $5 million per year.

Lifestyleco is run by an owner who is heavily involved in most aspects of the business. Few processes are in place and most of the goodwill is personal. Because of the heavy owner dependence the multiple is 2.5×. In addition there are inefficiencies in the business and unnecessary expenses. Free cash flow is $500,000 per year.

The second business, Valueco, is well run. Five years ago the owner started to delegate and invest in processes. The owner's goodwill has been transferred to the business. The result is that the multiple is now 5×. Valueco also has fewer expenses, meaning more free cash flow – $750,000. So let's look at the differences:

Lifestyleco
Free cash flow, $500,000; multiple, 2.5× = value of $1.25 million

Valueco
Free cash flow, $750,000; multiple, 5× = value of $3.75 million

Both businesses are the same size and have the same sales, but there is a big difference in value. As you approach retirement, which business would you rather have?

Seven Levels of Multiples

To really appreciate the range of multiples it's helpful to consider them in seven levels. I'm certain there are others but this is a good start:

1. Starting at the bottom, we have the owner-dependent, personal goodwill lifestyle business: the multiple is 2–4×. Jason Kwiatkowski, a CPA and a chartered business valuator, reviewed this chapter and offered this insight about Level 1:

   The bottom level could be a 0 multiple. I have seen situations where the earnings/cash flows have not been sufficient enough to justify a value in excess of the net book value of the company. It is also possible that no matter what the cash flows are, if they are completely owner-dependent it would be very difficult to find someone to pay anything for a historical cash flow stream that will completely go away when the owner goes away.

2. Next is the optimized business with good processes and enterprise goodwill: 3–6×.
3. To climb up we add strategic value. Strategic value can command a multiple of 6–10×.
4. You can take the company public through an initial public offering (IPO). An IPO may be valued at a 20–40× multiple.
5. Guaranteed investments such as GICs trade in today's market at multiples between 25× and 100×, meaning they have annual returns of 4% down to 1%.

6. In the rarified world of life science and technology start-ups multiples can't even be calculated. Facebook paid $19 billion for WhatsApp, which may not have had any free cash flow. How do you calculate that multiple? If the free cash flow of WhatsApp was just $1 the multiple would be 19,000,000,000×.

7. The last level of multiple growth lies in the not-so-rarified world of lifestyle business. It is called strategic growth. If a lifestyle business starts at the bottom and works its way to the top, with sustained strategic growth, its value growth is limitless. Steve Jobs started in his garage and Warren Buffett at his kitchen table. The point of all these multiples is that our humble goal of closing the value gap no longer seems out of reach. All we need is a good business foundation and a team to build the second and third floors of value.

The Third Element:
Strategic Growth – Capturing the Motion

In the introduction I promised that *strategic growth* blows the doors off *strategic value*. This section explains how.

Strategic growth is another way of saying long-term sustainable growth. We say *strategic* rather than sustainable because strategy is the tool we use to achieve sustainability. In addition to the ideas in this section, strategic growth relies on all the ideas in this book, especially those in Chapters 7 and 8 – employee engagement and leadership.

Strategic growth is similar to win-win. It is a martial art that requires superior skill. It is quality, not an add-on. Sun Tzu said, "All men see the tactics by which I conquer, but what none can see is the strategy out of which victory is evolved." To evolve victory, strategic growth must be considered as the very fabric of and reason for the existence of the business. Without it, you will not be able to hire your buyer.

Strategic *growth* must be distinguished from strategic *value*. Strategic value is the value a purchaser sees in acquiring your business. Strategic value is limited to the point in time of the sale. The difference is that strategic growth can capture many cycles of strategic value, not just the one that exists at the point of a valuation. Strategic growth captures the motion of the business.

But to grow the business you must resolve what Peter B. Brown, writing in *Forbes*, called the "entrepreneurial paradox":

Implementing an idea is where the entrepreneur often stumbles on the road to riches... About half of the companies that pass the financial screens to qualify as one of the best small companies in America one year will fail to repeat the next. Why?

It turns out that dealing with growth hurdles almost always requires the entrepreneur to think in ways that are *the exact opposite* of what initially made him a success. Why this is so becomes clear if you trace the route that all entrepreneurs take.

In the beginning, there is the idea. It comes from the entrepreneur. He thought of it and only he, at first, understands it. From there, the entrepreneur works to build a company. At first he makes all the decisions himself and does almost all the work – from product design to bookkeeping – alone. Most often, he doesn't have any choice.

It is the fact that the entrepreneur is the one best able to see the motion of the business that hampers growth. Entrepreneurs can't do everything themselves, and they shouldn't. But that is a difficult lesson to learn.

Strategic growth involves that difficult lesson. The point of strategic growth is to grow the business past the founder and into the shoes of the next generation of owners. This involves four interconnected features: growth rate; four spinning plates; core, segments and adjacencies; and acquisitions.

Growth Rate

Let's look at the first interconnected feature. What should your growth rate be? Consider the following annual growth rates for $1 million for 15 years.

Growth Rate of $1 Million	Value after 15 Years
5%	$2,079,000
10%	$4,157,000
15%	$8,137,000
20%	$15,407,000
25%	$28,421,000
30%	$51,185,000

The first thing that jumps out is the exponential effect of the compound interest curve over time. A return of 15% is four times the return at 5%. The return at 30% is 25 times the return at 5%.

What should the growth rate of your business be?

At the top of the chart, a return of 5% is only a little above Canada's historical inflation rate, which, according to Statistics Canada, was 3.26% from 1915 to 2010. At 5% growth, the business is almost standing still, providing no real return on the investment.

According to Canada Life the 60-year average return for the stock market from 1953 to 2012 was 9.8%. If the business is growing at only 10% you are not being properly rewarded for the work and effort you are putting in.

OK, so how high do we go? How about 30%?

A return of 30% puts you in league with the best-performing companies of all time. *The Breakthrough Company: How Everyday Companies Become Extraordinary Performers* is a book about an extensive five-year research effort to find the fastest growing companies from the Inc. 500 list. From thousands, the nine top-performing companies were chosen for in-depth study. Author Keith R. McFarland says, "In the fifteen years following their appearance on Inc.'s list of the 500 fastest growing companies, the median revenue of these nine companies grew from $14.4 million to more than $700 million." This represents an annual growth rate of almost exactly 30%.

Although such high rates are to be applauded they are not realistic for most businesses. In fact very high rates of growth can be dangerous and are a leading cause of premature business death.

Consider Garland Industries. Garland placed short-term workers at factories primarily to reduce reliance on unionized labor. Garland was more successful than most placement agencies because the front-line managers were recruited for an unusual skill – street fighting – which was necessary because union members often called them scabs.

Garland's profits grew at 50% per year but cash flow was a killer. Temp workers are paid every two weeks and the government wants payroll remittances. Factories paid Garland in 90 to 120 days or longer. Ironically it was Garland's profitability that killed it. Garland needed every dime it could find to finance an ever-growing payroll. But on paper Garland reported a large profit. At the end of each year there was a lot of tax to pay. Garland's accountants pushed off the tax bill for four years through a series of holding companies. A government tax audit concluded that three of the holding companies had no business purpose. Taxes for three of those four years became due NOW, plus penalties and interest. Garland could fight no more.

Looking at the table above, a growth rate of 10% does not seem to reward you for the effort of running your business. The next level, 15%, represents a real rate of return that is sustainable and has a reward element for the effort of managing the business. At a 15% growth rate the value of the business doubles every five years. As you can see from the chart a 15% growth rate for 15 years increases the value of a business by 800%, or 8×. This growth provides plenty of opportunity for the retiring owner to cash out and an incentive to the employees who are creating value.

Four Spinning Plates: Marketing, Operational Infrastructure, Human Resources and Finance

The second interconnected feature consists of four spinning plates. We saw from the Garland story that growth has to be managed and that the illusion of excess profits can kill a business.

The Ministry of Small Business in British Columbia published a 70-page guide called *Planning for Business Growth*. The guide explains that to grow you need to balance four essential aspects of business: marketing, operational infrastructure, human resources and finance. You need to be a bit of a busker to keep all those plates spinning at the same time.

Marketing has to spin out enough orders to sustain the growth. Then you have to process the orders. If your operational infrastructure can't properly process the orders, you get a bottleneck.

To avoid the bottleneck you need the right people in place to do the spinning. Jim Collins explains in *Good to Great*:

> One of the immutable laws of management physics is this: No company can grow revenues consistently faster than its ability to get enough of the right people to implement that growth and still become a great company. If your growth rate in revenues consistently outpaces your growth rate in people, you simply will not – indeed cannot – build a great company.

The fourth plate you have to spin is finance. You have to be able to finance the growth, which we saw that Garland could not do – at least not at the pace it was growing.

Core Business, Segments and Adjacencies

The third interconnected feature is developing your core business. A term related to core business is core competence. Long-term sustainable growth requires that you consistently win the business. To consistently win you have to be the best. Your core competence is what you do better than everyone else and from that core competence you grow your core business.

The question then becomes, the best at what? The way to be the best is to carefully choose the business you can win at. The answer is not always obvious. Railways were the dot-coms of the 19th century. Great fortunes were made connecting the continent. But thousands of railway companies disappeared in the 20th century as roads developed. Had the railway companies thought of their core business as transportation instead of railways they could have cashed in a second time.

Having a clear perception of what you do eliminates what you don't do. Knowing what you don't do is very important so that you don't waste resources.

You can grow your core business in three ways: the way you've always grown it, by expanding into *new market segments* and by growing into *adjacent businesses*.

An excellent study of the core business concept and the three ways to grow it is found in *Profit from the Core* by Chris Zook, a partner at Bain & Company. Zook did not start out with the core in mind, he undertook a study of thousands of businesses to see what the best long-term sustainable strategies were. It was only after this extensive study that he concluded that the most important *growth* strategy is to strengthen and defend your core business. Zook emphasizes that you should not focus on the newest or latest strategy; rather, you should identify your core business and focus on that.

Strengthening your core business involves three essential points:

1. Define your core (what you do) and your boundaries (what you don't do).
2. Identify what you do better than anyone else.
3. Assess whether your core business is operating at or near its business potential.

The first point – defining your core business – is often challenging for large businesses because they do many things. In many small businesses I walk into, defining what they do is not that hard simply because they don't do as many things.

The second point is your competitive advantage. Why do people choose to do business with you? Are you the last gas station for 100 miles? Do you have a recipe that can't be beat? Have you taken time to develop a network? Look at what has worked and why, and work on improving that.

The third point – whether the core business is operating at full potential – is interesting for a small business. A Fortune 500 company may already have a 30–40% market share so it's hard to increase in size significantly. Microsoft already owns 80% of the market for desktop operating systems, so how much more of the market can it get?

Smaller businesses have a lot more growth potential. Consider a small business in the consulting engineering business doing $1 million a year in sales. The market for consulting engineering is in the billions. Growing a well-run $1 million consulting business to a $10 million consulting business seems inevitable rather than impossible.

Jeff Bezos, CEO of Amazon.com, has an interesting take on what a core business is:

> I very frequently get the question: "what's going to change in the next 10 years?"... I almost never get the question: "what's not going to change in the next 10 years?" And I submit to you that that

second question is actually the more important of the two – because you can build a business strategy around the things that are stable in time… In our retail business, we know that customers want low prices and I know that's going to be true 10 years from now. They want fast delivery, they want vast selection… And so the effort we put into those things, spinning those things up, we know the energy we put into it today will still be paying off dividends for our customers 10 years from now. When you have something that you know is true, even over the long term, you can afford to put a lot of energy into it.

Bezos is saying that the core of Amazon's business is the core unchanging needs of Amazon's customers: low prices, fast delivery and selection. Amazon invests in improving those areas. Amazon's core business does not revolve around technology, it revolves around timeless customer needs.

A core business can grow through additional *market segments*. A market segment is a new group of identifiable consumers who will buy the core business's product. An example of finding a new market segment is to sell the same core product in new places. Some of the high-end luxury goods that sell on the runways in Milan also sell quite well in airports.

Different types of locations can represent different market segments. McDonald's restaurant took years to make the separate decisions to expand into downtowns, to highway cloverleafs and then to malls. Each decision required extensive market research and different strategies. Each of these expansions represents the growth of a core business through different market segments.

A core business can also grow through an *adjacent business*. An adjacent business appears different from your core but is logically connected and overlaps in important ways. Recall the references to strategic or synergistic purchasers creating value by adding your business to theirs. An adjacent business is also strategic or synergistic because you use a lot of the infrastructure you have already built to create a brand new business.

Let's consider an example of a business that was not adjacent. Polaris, the snowmobile company, expanded into personal watercraft – Jet Skis – to keep its plant running in the summer. Jet Skis seemed to be a logical extension of the snowmobile business. After a year or so Polaris realized that the watercraft market was not an adjacent business. The propulsion system and the sales distribution system were different. Addressing these differences required significant new investment and risk. Surprisingly, there was little synergy between Jet Skis and snowmobiles.

A few years later Polaris hit a home run when it expanded into four-wheel-drive all-terrain vehicles. ATVs have the same drive train and sales distribution system as snowmobiles – synergy galore.

The McDonald's story offers a compelling illustration of the difference between market segments and adjacent business. As we saw, McDonald's grew through market segments, but it also grew through a very important adjacent business. McDonald's was a lunch and dinner restaurant selling burgers, shakes and fries. The decision to add a breakfast menu took 10 years.

Breakfast was a new business that depended on an entirely new menu and a new supply chain. As it turned out, the McDonald's breakfast business *was* adjacent to its lunch business. Breakfast was adjacent because it appealed to the same customers, through the same locations – locations that would otherwise be empty at breakfast time. Breakfast added 25% to same-store sales and amazed the executives. For a chain as large as McDonald's the adjacent breakfast business added revenue equivalent to 8,000 locations without the real estate cost. It literally built an entire chain of breakfast restaurants without lifting a hammer. Now that's synergy.

What is adjacent or synergistic is not always obvious. Warren Buffet is in 77 adjacent businesses, not because they all relate to a core product but because they all relate to a core strategy. Buffett buys only businesses he can understand, such as commodity businesses, or strong cash businesses, such as insurance companies, with proven track records and trusted management teams. He also has a blend of companies designed to ride a cyclical economy. Any company fitting his parameters is adjacent to his core.

Acquisitions

The fourth interconnected feature of strategic growth is acquisitions. Eugene Merfeld, Gary Schine and David Annis, authors of *Strategic Acquisition: A Smarter Way to Grow a Small or Medium Size Company*, explain the benefits of acquisitions:

Growth through acquisition is a quicker, cheaper, and far less risky proposition than the tried and true methods of expanded marketing and sales efforts. Acquisition offers a myriad of other advantages such as easier financing and instant economies of scale. The competitive advantages too are formidable, ranging from catching one's competition off guard, to instant market penetration even in areas where you may currently be weak, to the elimination of a competitor(s) through its acquisition. It is quite common for a company to buy another to take better advantage of each other's distribution channels...

The benefits of growth through acquisition are hardly limited to marketing. It is typically easier to finance growth via acquisition than via more traditional routes of expansion... Lenders and investors are more impressed by real financials than with projections based on business plans, no matter how positive they may be. Furthermore, a whole otherwise non-existent form of financing is available through the common practice of seller financing.

In spite of these advantages you have to remember that 50–70% of acquisitions fail to show a return on the cost of capital. To be successful you should focus on acquisitions that increase the size of the core business or add market segments or adjacent businesses to the core. Acquisitions in non-core business areas are historically very risky.

As stated above *employee engagement* and *leadership* are also necessary elements of strategic growth but owing to their complexity I've given each its own chapter.

The 32× Fair Market Value Algorithm

To conclude this chapter I will set out a mathematical formula for increasing the FMV of your company by 32×. It takes time, but it really should be a goal for all business owners. Even if you get only half or a quarter of the way to this goal you will have a fantastic result.

It should be noted that Industry Canada says the average annual growth rate for businesses is 3.6%. If this were some type of cap above which a business could not grow it would be irresponsible to even mention 32× growth in FMV. But remember that that growth rate includes a lot of large businesses that simply can't grow like small ones can. And more importantly it includes the hundreds of thousands of lifestyle businesses whose owners do not understand value creation and make no effort to grow.

Further – and more to the point – 3.6% is not going to cut it for the kind of value creation we need to enable you to hire your buyer. So if 3.6% is our absolute cap I have just wasted a bunch of trees. I do not expect that every lifestyle business owner will adopt this philosophy, but for those who "get it," I have faith that some of you will be able to pull it off.

The 32× FMV algorithm works like this. Let's say you have a typical lifestyle business with a lot of personal goodwill and you have never paid attention to value creation. Based on your investigations you have decided that you have free cash flow of $400,000 and a multiple of 2.5× ($1 million FMV).

What you are trying to achieve in 15 years is to multiply the FMV of your business by 32× what it is worth today (leading to a $32 million FMV). This goal should provide abundant cash for you to retire and a sufficient incentive for the employees who are going to assist in the value creation.

To get to $32 million you need to double $1 million five times: to $2 million, $4 million, $8 million, $16 million and finally to $32 million. Each of these doublings is a result of increases in free cash flow or the multiple. The following hypothetical case gives you an idea of how this might work.

The first doubling is 15% growth for five years. If we grow our free cash flow at 15% per year for five years we double it, which doubles FMV. Free cash flow growth comes from a combination of expense reduction and earnings growth. This is what five years of growth at 15% looks like:

Today	$1,000,000
Year 1	$1,150,000
Year 2	$1,322,000
Year 3	$1,520,000
Year 4	$1,749,000
Year 5	$2,011,000

The second doubling comes from the multiple. Converting personal goodwill into enterprise goodwill and optimizing business systems can double the multiple from 2.5× to 5×, which in turn doubles FMV. Let's assume it takes seven years, starting in Year 1, to get everything in place to double our multiple.

By Year 10 the third doubling has come from 15% growth in free cash flow for five more years.

By Year 14 we are now a fully professional company that has an FMV in excess of $10 million. We have also had a long track record of consistent growth and plans are in place to demonstrate future growth. Company management understands strategic growth. This makes the company attractive to professional buyers, which gives us a shot at the fourth doubling: doubling our multiple again from 5× to 10×, which once again doubles the FMV.

By Year 15 another five years of 15% growth in free cash flow doubles the FMV for the fifth time, arriving at the magic 32× FMV. The chart below provides a summary.

	Action	Years from Now	Fair Market Value
1st doubling	Grow free cash flow for 5 years at 15%	Year 5	$2 million
2nd doubling	Grow multiple from 2.5× to 5×	Year 7	$4 million
3rd doubling	Grow free cash flow for 5 more years at 15%	Year 10	$8 million
4th doubling	Grow multiple from 5× to 10×	Year 14	$16 million
5th doubling	Grow free cash flow for 5 more years at 15%	Year 15	$32 million

To repeat, multiplying value by 32× over 15 years seems fantastical and hopelessly unrealistic to some – and for some it may be. But many others have done this and more. The point of this section is to give you an understanding of how the algorithm could work. Now let's move on to the last two chapters about strategic growth: engaging the employees and your buyer so they can help you create that value, and understanding the leadership skills you will need to lead your buyer team.

Chapter 7

Employee Engagement: We're Great

The Importance of Employees

IN MANY LIFESTYLE BUSINESSES employees *are not* of crucial importance. They simply carry out tasks according to detailed instructions; they can be replaced. In a strategic growth company, employees take on a much more significant role.

In 1997, William A. Sahlman, author of the widely read *Harvard Business Review* article "How to Write a Great Business Plan," reflected on his experience of having read thousands of plans. His advice was not to take a lot of time on the financial sections – all plans say the company will achieve $50 million in sales by Year 3. His advice is to focus on getting the team right. "Do what experienced venture capitalists do, and skip immediately to the section outlining 'the team': who was going to be involved, what their track record is."

Herb Kelleher, cofounder and former CEO of Southwest Airlines, was asked to explain his company's competitive advantage. His response: "Our people. We take good care of them, they take good care of our customers, and our customers take good care of our shareholders."

At Four Seasons Hotels & Resorts, founder Isadore Sharp instituted the golden rule and ensured that his employees were very well treated. His rationale is very straightforward: guests interact with hotel employees. The extraordinarily high level of service that guests at Four Seasons receive reflects the treatment the employees receive. Sharp believed that the company had to walk the talk. To simply state a value about treating employees well and then not follow through would make employees cynical and would be worse than having no values at all.

Do Employee Buyouts Work?

In 2001, Rod Reynolds, president of Roynat Capital Inc., a bank specializing in business lending, wrote an article entitled "How to Save the Family Business." What he reports about the success of employee-led buyouts is as astounding as the failure rate of mergers.

> A family-owned business is at serious risk when a son or daughter takes the CEO's chair. In our experience as a merchant bank, we've found that 70% of family businesses don't survive to the next generation. The odds are little better – just 50/50 – when a business is sold to an outside buyer. In contrast, successions involving leveraged employee buyouts, supported by key managers, succeed in about 80% of cases.

> These estimates are supported by US studies, and the numbers reveal a simple truth that financial institutions involved in financing the acquisitions of private businesses have known for years: Those with direct experience in a business are its best bet after a transition of ownership.

In *Good to Great* Jim Collins discusses whether great companies need to look outside for new leaders or whether employees should be considered as candidates.

> The evidence does not support the idea that you need an outside leader to come in and shake up the place to go from good to great. In fact, going for a high-profile outside change agent is negatively correlated with a sustained transformation from good to great.

> Ten out of eleven good-to-great CEOs came from inside the company, three of them by family inheritance. The comparison companies turned to outsiders with six times greater frequency – yet they failed to produce sustained great results.

In short, more important than *skin* in the game, employees provide *skill* in the game.

Another overlooked aspect is that a job is critical to an employee. I had a discussion with an investment banker from a very large New York investment firm. We were discussing employee ownership. He told me the key to performance was a good CEO: "They get paid so much because when they have that much at stake they really produce." I replied that employees have just as much at stake: a $50,000 salary is the difference between being comfortable and living on the street.

· · · · · · · · · · · · · ·

Successions involving leveraged employee buyouts, supported by key managers, succeed in about 80% of cases.

· · · · · · · · · · · · · ·

There is someone who agrees with me. In Chapter 4 we reviewed the research by the company the Great Place to Work Institute. That research says the number one lesson for leaders who want to build a great workplace is to remember this: "Your employees' lives are at stake."

Incentive Plans

OK. So how do I engage employees – pay them more?

No, paying more doesn't work. You could go into a company and give everyone a 50% raise and nothing would change, if for no other reason than the fact that nobody would know that anything *should* change. Even if they knew change was required they wouldn't know what to do. Incentives can be like junk food. If incentives are disconnected from performance they are just empty calories with no nutritional benefit.

The idea of incentives is that the *penalty* of not receiving the incentive at the end of the year is, by itself, sufficient motivation to govern the attitude and behavior of employees every day throughout the year. This doesn't work.

For an incentive to have an effect it has to work as part of a larger engagement strategy. If incentives are just written on paper, if they're simply a term in a contract and are not a part of the culture, they're not part of the fabric of the company and they don't work. Brad Hams explains in his book *Ownership Thinking: How to End Entitlement and Create a Culture of Accountability, Purpose, and Profit* that beyond being ineffective, incentive plans can actually damage a company.

In a typical incentive plan, there is little connection between what employees actually do and the incentive dollars they receive or don't receive. So what happens? They get to the end of a quarter and receive a big bonus check. They don't know why, but, of course, they are happy to receive this "gift." Perhaps they receive bonuses for several consecutive quarters…

Eventually there will be a quarter with poor business performance. Employees don't know this because they have not been seeing financial information and have not been engaged. The only thing they know is that they will not be getting a bonus this quarter. What do you suppose they are thinking now? Given how they have been conditioned, they are most likely thinking that they are getting screwed… The outcome is (1) little or no change in behavior, (2) a new expense, and (3) an angry and ungrateful workforce.

The point is that giving incentives to employees without financial education and engagement can be more harmful than giving them no incentives at all.

Financial Education

The solution is that rather than focusing on incentives you should focus on engagement. Engagement is a strategy that works every day. The first practical step toward engaging employees is to educate them about how the company works and what its financial results are. Open-book management is a management style designed to educate employees about the finances of the company. This idea directly contradicts the standard advice to make sure employees never have access to financial information.

How far you go in releasing information depends on the company. In some companies the books are opened and financial statements and financial information is shared with employees. Some companies go so far as to release salary information.

But *open book* does not mean you have to share everything. What it really means is that employees should understand what makes a company successful financially and how they contribute to that success. The real point is that they receive meaningful education and sufficient communication to know what the important value metrics are and what makes the business valuable. Most importantly, they should understand which of their choices will or will not create value. Freedom empowers them to make the choice and financial education empowers their responsibility to make the right choice.

Donna Fenn, contributing editor for *Inc.* magazine, wrote the book *Alpha Dogs: How Your Small Business Can Become a Leader of the Pack* about six companies that lead. One of them is specialty food store chain Dorothy Lane Markets, which leads its category in areas such as employee programs, customer relations and technology. Its profits have been as high as 4%, more than double the industry average, and its staff turnover is well below the industry norm.

One practice that Dorothy Lane CEO Norman Mayne believes in is spending an hour talking to every new entry-level employee about company culture, industry margins, customer retention, demographics and the competition. Mayne has been doing this for 20 years. Fenn describes the Dorothy Lane financial education process:

"On a $25 grocery order, how much profit do you think we make?" [Mayne] asks them. "Is it $12.50, $7.50, $2.50, or 75 cents?"... They're genuinely flabbergasted when he tells them the answer: 75 cents.

Dorothy Lane has an intranet that Mayne thinks is "the best in the industry." Every employee can log on and get a good look at the company's key numbers... "If you're a delivery guy in the back room, you probably know what our revenues are," says Kent Dimbath, Dorothy Lane's CFO... "Information is power, so I want the people who work here to know as much as they can," says Mayne...

"From 2001 to 2003, our health care expenses went from $400,000 to $800,000 to $1.4 million," explains Mayne... The company had to reduce some of its health coverage and ask employees to foot the bill for a greater percentage... because his employees had access to the company's financials, they understood why the decision was made... "There's a level of trust, and people say, okay, we really need to cut costs – we know you're not lying to us."

Randal Root, of Root Learning, asks that we imagine what would happen if everyone in the company were to think like business owners. In his white paper "Creating a Company of 'Owners'" he asks us to consider 10 key questions. These four provide a sense of the overall direction necessary to develop an ownership mentality among employees:

» What if every person in your organization really understood the big picture, including the economic, technological, competitive and market realities of your business?

» What if all of your people had an understanding of your strategy far more focused and meaningful than murky visions and missions?

» What if they understood your organization's core competencies, knowing exactly what skills would be required to achieve your strategic goals?

» What if they realized how slim your margins are and how they could help them grow?

William C. Taylor and Polly G. LaBarre wrote *Mavericks at Work: Why the Most Original Minds in Business Win*, a *Wall Street Journal* bestseller, about a number of very successful one-of-a-kind companies. They found at least one principle common to all these businesses: "Companies that are serious about understanding what makes their people tick, equip their people with a serious understanding of what makes the company itself tick."

. . . .

Educating employees about how the company is growing value should be part of a wider and deeper continuous learning and growth environment.

. . . .

As an example they talk about Dick Resch, president of KI, which sells sophisticated office furniture to large technology firms. Resch said the 3,500 KI employees have immersed themselves in the company's strategy and operations. KI couldn't engage so deeply with its elite, demanding customers if its employees weren't so deeply engaged in the intricacies of the business.

Taylor and LaBarre describe the monthly financial information meetings at KI as a maverick innovation and explain why:

> At KI, employees get access to information in another one of Dick Resch's maverick innovations – a monthly roll-up-the-sleeves-and-look-at-the-numbers gathering... a three-hour blizzard of data, questions, market intelligence, wisecracks, and history lessons that was intense, entertaining, and (for a visitor at least) exhausting...
>
> It felt like the office furniture equivalent of an air-traffic control tower – lots of people making sense of lots of data in very little time... The participants, regardless of rank or seniority, threw themselves into the fray...
>
> KI can be more agile in the marketplace because it has built such a highly engaged, highly informed workplace.

Open-book management is not an add-on; it is not a cure. Simply opening the books by itself does nothing and may be harmful. Used properly, however, open-book management is a step in creating deeper, more fundamental employee engagement through education about what makes the company work. Educating employees about how the company is growing value should be part of a wider and deeper continuous learning and growth environment.

Another frequently used term is "participative management." It's the outcome of financial education. When employees are educated they have the choice to participate in the management of the firm. This is how they can exercise responsibility.

Employee Ownership

The next step in engagement, after financial education, is employee ownership. Once again, by itself employee ownership, like incentives or opening the books, does nothing. Each of these elements must be part of a deeper, more meaningful plan of employee engagement.

In 1973 a couple of hundred pulp and paper workers in Témiscaming, Quebec, decided not to give up on their company. It was not just their jobs; the entire town was on the line. Employee-owned Tembec was created through the efforts of the community and its people. Frank Dottori and three other executives led the determined struggle to save the mill. The company was founded on an unprecedented relationship between management, unionized employees, the community and various levels of government.

Carol Beatty is an associate professor at Queen's University's School of Business and author of *Employee Ownership: The New Source of Competitive Advantage*. She describes being taken aback when tough-as-nails Tembec founder Dottori said that employee ownership gives him a 15% cost advantage over his traditional rivals. Dottori explains: "Every employee must be a shareholder and ownership must be significant enough to give employees a real sense of ownership and responsibility. Management style must also be different in such an employee enterprise. Management doesn't have rights in our companies, we have responsibilities."

* * *

By itself employee ownership, like incentives or opening the books, does nothing. Each of these elements must be part of a deeper, more meaningful plan of employee engagement.

* * *

Tembec believes its unique culture has stimulated innovation, entrepreneurship and a distinct competitiveness, allowing it to grow from its original mill in Témiscaming with a few hundred employees into the international company it is today. At the end of 2004, the last full year Dottori worked for Tembec, the company had more than 55 manufacturing units and approximately 11,000 employees, gross sales of C$3.7 billion and assets of nearly $4 billion.

Employee Stock Ownership Programs

Employee stock ownership programs (ESOPs) were developed in the US based on specific legislation that provides substantial tax incentives. The term is also used in Canada but there is no specific legislation for it as there is in the US. In Canada an ESOP can use stock options and can also provide substantial tax benefits.

A 2007 *Profit* magazine article, "The Lure of ESOPs," said,

Smart CEOs are always on the lookout for tools that will help attract, motivate and retain top talent, especially in today's ever-tightening labour market. This year's survey of Canada's Fastest-Growing Companies shows that PROFIT 100 leaders consider... ESOPS part of the solution. Almost half (47%) of them run ESOPS and say they attract and keep workers, facilitate succession planning and boost productivity.

In 1987 the Toronto Stock Exchange conducted a study of companies with meaningful employee ownership. This study revealed that these companies have

» 123% higher five-year growth
» 95% higher net profit margin
» 92% higher return on total equity
» 65% higher return on capital
» 24% higher productivity

In *Mavericks at Work* Taylor and LaBarre describe the KI ownership plan:

> Back in 1981, shares in the company were worth less than a dime each. By the end of 2004, shares of KI were valued at an all-time high of nearly $27. That's a 24-year compound annual rate of return of more than 30 percent... It's no surprise that managers and rank-and-file employees are eager to adopt an "ownership mind-set."

KI is now a company of owner-employees who clearly understand how the company operates. Taylor and LaBarre describe that as "a phenomenal competitive engine."

It's important to repeat that ESOPs by themselves do not engage employees. Engagement comes from a concerted effort that may or may not include an ESOP. In fact, there have been large ESOP failures. United Airlines went bankrupt after employees gave up wages and benefits in exchange for shares under an ESOP. There had been complaints that the ESOP was not open to all employees. Some employees got better benefits than others and the ESOP had only a five-year life, after which it was wound up. It was simply an add-on. All management did was set up a temporary ESOP without consultation; nothing else at the company changed. When United Airlines failed, management pointed at the ESOP and said, "we told you so."

In spite of some failures, the National Center for Employee Ownership (NCEO) in California argues that "Researchers agree the 'case is closed' on employee ownership and corporate performance. Findings this consistent are very unusual. We can say with certainty that when ownership and participative management are combined, substantial gains result. Ownership or participation alone, however, have at best spotty or short-term results."

As an example of what it takes to succeed with an ESOP, the NCEO tells the story of Jackson's Hardware:

> Jackson's Hardware started an ESOP in 1989 and has been 100% employee owned for over a decade. It looks like an old-fashioned hardware store. Its large pink building opens early in the morning when contractors from around the Bay Area come to shop... There are lots of experts, however – Jackson's takes out regular newspaper ads filled with pictures of its 70 employee owners highlighting their long years of service.

> Jackson's is an open-book company. Weekly and monthly sales figures are posted for everyone to see. Employees know the financials and receive bonuses based on them. There are meetings about ways to improve the bottom line, and their ideas are taken seriously by CEO Bill Loskutoff.

Three elements that seem to combine to work very well together when it comes to engaging employees are open-book management, participative management and employee ownership. In 1987, *Harvard Business Review* published an article entitled "How Well Is Employee Ownership Working?" This article reported that companies with ownership cultures grow 8–11% faster than would be expected if they did not. The authors of the article state,

> By the late 1990s, the word had gotten out that the leading employee ownership companies were those with open-book

management and highly participative decision making. Leaders and employee owners at these companies became enthusiastic evangelists for this new way to work. Not only were they making more money, but they were having more fun doing it.

Going back to our strategic growth rate for a moment, if an employee ownership culture can add 8–11% growth, we are a lot closer to 15% than we would be without it.

Converting Personal Goodwill

An interesting aspect of employee engagement is that it allows you to convert your non-transferable personal goodwill into capital gain income as you sell off portions of your business.

A good example comes from Randy, a high-performing consultant in the assembly line automation business. Randy had been in business for 30 years and had many contacts. He made a very good income and had more work than he was able to handle. He started to plan when he was 60.

The problem was that if Randy stopped working he stopped earning, and if he left the business most of his clients would stop earning too. Randy's business was not transferable – it was based on personal goodwill.

Randy's personal goodwill was like the energy produced by a light bulb: only the light can be used; the heat is wasted. Randy's personal goodwill attracted more work than he could do; any work he couldn't get to was a wasted opportunity. What Randy needed was a plan to capture that wasted opportunity and convert it into free cash flow.

Instead of selling his company Randy decided to capture his wasted goodwill. He decided to hire a new consultant every year for four years. He went after the best young consultants he could find and offered them top salaries. He explained that he was one of the best in the business and he could teach them to be as well. Basically, he could use his personal goodwill, which would otherwise be wasted, to bake them into a good practice.

After the young consultants had been with the company for three years Randy proposed to sell them the shares of the company. Randy's plan was to slowly transfer 75% of the company over seven years; he would sell the last 25% when he was 75. After that, even though he would no longer own shares he would consider whether he was still interested in part-time work.

The key that would allow him to do that was, of course, to engage his consultants, to educate them about how the business worked and grew in value and to allow them to participate in the management of the company. And then as they built the value, he would sell it to them.

Here's the magic part:

The price that each new consultant paid was 75% of what the entire company was worth when it was just Randy by himself. That means Randy would end up selling the company for three to four times what he could have sold it for before he started hiring his buyers. In addition, he would receive a similar amount in extra profit from the work of the additional consultants, meaning he ended up with more than seven times the amount he would have received had he simply sold.

Where did this extra value come from? The price that the new consultants paid to buy the shares was based on the value they themselves created after joining the company. In addition, they generated new profits that Randy would keep at first and then later share in, until he finally sold out.

Randy himself reduced his hours by 50% but was still able to pull in almost the same salary because he no longer had to carry out administrative tasks. Randy focused exclusively on the best, most difficult cases, which in turn made the company and the other consultants look good.

The result was that Randy could come and go as he pleased and cherry-pick the assignments he wanted. If he wanted to go to Arizona for four months in the winter or if he had a health issue the company would keep humming along.

Golder Three-Peats as Top 10 Employer in Canada

This is the story of Canadian engineering firm Golder Associates. Golder, a little like Google, is a large lifestyle company for engineers seeking challenging work in a collegial environment. Profit maximization is not the company's only goal. Golder used employee engagement and many of the ideas we have been discussing to climb from a three-person firm to a firm of 8,000 engineers.

Golder was started in Toronto in 1960 by Hugh Golder, Victor Milligan, Larry Soderman and John Seychuk. One night Golder, Milligan and Soderman were sitting around a kitchen table discussing how to grow the company. They decided that giving shares to employees was the best way to grow.

In 2011 the company published an e-book about its history, *Conversations on Our First 50 Years*. An important point Golder makes is that employee share ownership is not enough. There must also be a commitment to employee culture, especially for those employees who do not own shares.

In the years leading up to 1996 Golder was having employee problems that it didn't even recognize. The company was working well for the higher-ups but not so much for the rank and file. In 1996, Golder hired Hal Hamilton as president. The Golder history offers his description of the problem:

> We weren't making money, we weren't selling shares. We had hired this external company (Human Factors) that had looked at our psychology and said, "You guys are really screwed up. You need to get this sorted out."... No change would happen unless I, as the President, drove it.

> The first thing that was striking was a disconnect between the senior team and the junior team...

> Secondly... Golder had a very aggressive culture which showed up in the oppositional scale of the organisational cultural inventory as almost off the chart... That, linked to the push for professional perfectionism, which was one of the other scales, tended to make it very difficult for anyone to participate in a conversation without feeling that they were being unnecessarily challenged – nothing was good enough, and they couldn't do anything right...

Golder conducted surveys and realized that it had an additional problem. The surveys revealed that Golder was lacking in the simple human courtesy of recognition. Like an overly ambitious parent relentlessly driving a child for more and more achievement, Golder was missing important human skills.

Once the human skill issues were identified Golder made a serious long-term commitment to fixing them. This is how Golder's book describes the ambiance and objectives of the firm now:

> People don't come to Golder to get wealthy. They come to Golder because they want a home. A large percentage of the people in Golder are very proud of the fact that they are "lifers."...

> Its objectives were, first and foremost, to do good work, second to seek challenging work wherever it might be found and only third to make money at it (regarded by some as a consequence rather than a driver).

In February 2014, for the third year in a row Golder was honored by the *Financial Post* as one of Canada's Ten Best Companies to Work For.

The Balanced Scorecard

One of the management tools that Golder Associates adopted during its 1996 crisis was the Balanced Scorecard (BSC).

The editors of *Harvard Business Review* selected the BSC concept as one of the most influential management ideas of the past 75 years. The official figures vary slightly but the Gartner Group suggests that over 50% of large US firms have adopted it.

In 1992 Robert Kaplan and David Norton developed an innovative solution to a significant problem that plagued management: managers did not understand how to properly make decisions.

At that time decisions were made on the basis of their financial impact. Is this a profitable project? Does this manager's department generate profit? The problem with this profit-centric approach is that it misses the problems inherent in certain decisions. For instance, Gibson Guitars, which had for decades been producing the best guitars on the market, was sold to a cement company. The cement company instituted many cost-cutting measures that for five years produced record profits; however, that profit came at a heavy cost. Customers were disappointed in the low-quality products produced and Gibson was in danger of losing its reputation. Eventually quality returned as the number one priority even if it came at a cost.

It was to this one-dimensional thinking that Kaplan and Norton turned their minds in 1992. The authors developed a BSC, a multidimensional performance measurement system that gives top managers a fast but comprehensive view of their business. The BSC includes financial measures that reveal the results of previous actions. But it adds three other important measures:

1. **Customer satisfaction:** This measure would have quickly identified the Gibson Guitar problem.
2. **Internal processes:** This measure relates to the way a decision will affect the internal processes of the company. Cutting staff may save money, but it also may harm the ability to process orders. If a company were to consider an acquisition it should ask itself, can we handle this additional responsibility with our existing management?
3. **The organization's ability to learn and improve:** In other words, do financial measures, such as cost cutting, impair the company's ability to learn and improve? Does an expenditure add to the company's ability to learn and improve?

None of these categories is the trump card but filtering decisions through these different lenses results in "balanced" decisions. This is how *HBR* describes the concept:

> The traditional financial performance measures that worked for the industrial era are out of sync with the skills organizations are trying to master. Frustrated by these inadequacies, some managers have abandoned financial measures like return on equity and earnings per share. "Make operational improvements, and the numbers will follow," the argument goes. But managers want a balanced presentation of measures that allow them to view the company from several perspectives at once…

> The Balanced Scorecard helps managers look at their businesses from four essential perspectives and answer some important questions: How do customers see us? What must we excel at? Can we continue to improve and create value? How do we appear to shareholders? By looking at all of these parameters, managers

can determine whether improvements in one area have come at the expense of another. Armed with that knowledge… executives can glean a complete picture of where the company stands – and where it's headed.

There is no one correct way to use the BSC. Every company has a different blend of traits, capabilities and deliverables and uses that mix differently. The point of the BSC is to indicate that profit maximization and financial results by themselves are insufficient and ineffective measures of company performance.

A scorecard could look like this:

BALANCED SCORECARD

The idea of the BSC is similar to the four spinning plates necessary for strategic growth referred to in Chapter 6. A BSC looks at four spinning measures in the company and asks how each influences the other. This type of balanced thinking works well with the type of Integrative Thinking that the Rotman School of Management's Roger Martin believes is necessary for developing strategy and overcoming paradox. It was this type of balanced approach that allowed Golder to overcome its lack of people skills and become a great employer. Golder still uses the BSC approach today.

Hire Your Buyer: Eight Advantages

In addition to the fact that employee-led buyouts have a significantly higher survival rate, there are eight advantages to hiring your buyer that are not available when you just sell your business.

1. You Have More Control over the Type of Buyer You Work With

"Hire your buyer" has a very wide meaning. The idea is that instead of selling your business in an external sale to a buyer you don't know, you are actively taking control of the process to maximize your value through an internal transfer.

An internal transfer could be to children, existing employees, partners or anyone already connected with your business. If the person or people are already in your business, "hire" means that you want to view them differently than you have before. Consider what's required of a potential owner and objectively assess whether that person has the skills required – in other words, you're going to act as if you're about to hire someone to take over the business.

If after you make your assessment you decide you do not already have the right people in place, you can actually search for and hire someone to take over your business or to get it ready for the big sale.

2. Due Diligence Is Unnecessary

When you sell to an insider, that person already knows the business and its risks. There may be due diligence in terms of the financial statements but it will be substantially less than what someone who does not know anything about your business would require.

3. You Design the Terms

When you hire your buyer you are in control of the design of the game. You get to set all the terms and you don't have to worry about satisfying an external buyer.

4. It's Win-Win

In a business sale the process is essentially adversarial even if politely so. The buyer's lawyers are worried about being scammed, so the process is lengthy and can be painful.

When you hire your buyer you focus on building a win-win scenario. This is a very different dynamic, one that focuses on building a Stage 4 trust relationship rather than struggling to meet the demands of a Stage 3 negotiation.

5. There's No Risk of Sale Failure

If you hire your buyer you set the agenda and the terms so there's no risk that the sale agreement will not be signed. There is always a risk that the plans may not work out but these are business risks, not risks of the sale process.

6. You Can Sell Shares

When you hire your buyer you can sell shares and earn capital gains. In Canada, this allows you to claim the $800,000 capital gains exemption. If you plan it right, every member of your family may be able to claim this exemption.

7. Price Is Based on Fair Market Value Plus Buyer-Created Value

This statement makes no sense in the traditional business buy-sell transaction. No lawyer would agree that her buyer client share the value they create. However, in the hire your buyer transaction that is exactly what happens. If the succession process is properly managed the buyer will be responsible for the activities necessary to add value to the business. The owner gets to share in the value created by the buyer, not just at the time of the sale but over an extended period. This is not unfair; remember, the entire point is that the owner has created a solid foundation on which the team can build value. The whole point of the exercise is to share. Depending on your value creation plan there may be substantially more money paid out over time. If value creation is possible and you have the right team, you could get much more money than you previously thought possible.

8. Ownership and Control Transfer over Five to 20 Years

The business will still be yours for between five and 20 years. You still have an active business investment that can grow substantially in value while you slow down and pull yourself out of the company.

Employee engagement is the critical crucial step in a hire your buyer strategy. Engagement consists of a combination of educating employees, having them actively participate in managing the company and giving them a stake in the outcome that they pay for with skill in the game. Employee ownership is especially useful in business succession because as the employees are acquiring shares, you (as the owner) are being paid out. The trick is to design a formula built on value creation that will satisfy everybody's needs.

The next chapter deals with the role of the owner. The type of deep engagement that combines all the elements discussed in this chapter arises only through leadership. The entrepreneur has to step up and lead the buyer team.

Chapter 8

Entrepreneur Engagement: Leadership

What Does It Mean to Be a Leader?

EMPLOYEE ENGAGEMENT is very widely discussed on the Internet, garnering at least 2.3 million Google hits, and it has given rise to an industry of consultants. According to Wikipedia an engaged employee is "one who is fully absorbed by and enthusiastic about their work and so takes positive action to further the organization's reputation and interests."

What about the entrepreneur? Shouldn't the entrepreneur also be engaged? And if so, what does entrepreneur engagement mean?

Searching for a definition, entrepreneur engagement gets only 6,470 hits and many of these are about engaging the entrepreneur in education programs, not in the business. I couldn't find a definition, so let's build our own, starting with the "fully absorbed" definition of engaged employee. In contrast to "I'm great and fully absorbed in myself," the engaged entrepreneur says, "We're great and I'm fully absorbed in the business." The difference in definitions is that an entrepreneur is not an employee, so the only position left open to the engaged entrepreneur is that of leader.

Entrepreneurs, however, are not naturally leaders. Most control and direct their helpers. One of the big problems that prevents entrepreneurs from being leaders is the shot at the buzzer. A buzzer beater is one of the most exciting moments in sport, a dramatic basketball shot that arcs through the air while the game-ending buzzer sounds. If it goes in, it's a win. If it doesn't, it's a loss.

Keith R. McFarland, author of *The Breakthrough Company*, conducted The Attentional and Interpersonal Style (TAIS) personality test on 250 CEOs from the Inc. 500 list. He determined that entrepreneurs differed from large-firm CEOs in a number of ways. One of these ways is the buzzer beater:

> If there is a shot at the buzzer – they want to be the one to take it: According to our TAIS results, entrepreneurs tested extremely high on their ability to perform well under pressure – scoring 45 percent higher than CEOs of larger firms… Entrepreneurs also scored highly on their need for control. In other words, when the game is on the line, delegation is the furthest thing from an entrepreneur's mind: He or she not only expects to take the game-winning shot, he or she needs to.

During the off-season, basketball great Kobe Bryant used to shoot 2,000 practice shots a day. He was the National Basketball Association scoring leader in 2006 and 2007 but his team, the L.A. Lakers, didn't do so well. As the team leader, Bryant realized that to win the championship he had to pass the ball. 2007 was the last year he was scoring champion. In 2009 the Lakers won the ring. In Game 2 of the 2010 Western Conference finals, Bryant made a career high of 13 assists. The Lakers went on to win the championship for a second year in a row. Entrepreneurs hog the ball; leaders rely on the team to take the shot at the buzzer.

Definition of Leadership

There is no single universally accepted definition of leadership. There is no scientific approach that can tell us with certainty the right way to lead. Chef Gordon Ramsay, business magnate Donald Trump and TV host Jerry Springer have all created a lot of value by loudly trumpeting "I'm great, you're not." But what they really have are lifestyle businesses based on fantastically outsized personal goodwill. In my definition they are not leading, they are directing. Remove the main attraction and the tent collapses.

One of the questions Jim Collins explored in *Good to Great* was whether leadership mattered. He and his team made conscious efforts not to have a leadership bias. Collins concluded, to his surprise, that in *great* companies, leadership actually mattered more than he and the team originally thought. Even more surprising was that the leaders at all 11 great companies he studied shared a consistent style, which he labeled Level 5 leadership.

· · · · · · · · · · · · · · ·

Entrepreneurs hog the ball; leaders rely on the team to take the shot at the buzzer.

· · · · · · · · · · · · · · ·

Level 5 leaders are not the showboat, big-hair Donald Trump types. Rather, they are the humble coaching types who show unwavering resolve.

Humility is a leadership paradox. The definition of humility can be confusing: a modest or low view of one's own importance; humbleness. How does a low view translate into a great company? The answer is the second quality of Level 5 leaders: unwavering resolve. Theirs is not a humility born of lack of confidence. It is a humility born in battle and forged in tragedy and loss – an exhausted realization that they are neither more nor less, they just lead and are grateful to those who follow.

Collins describes the humility paradox:

> It is very important to grasp that Level 5 leadership is not just about humility and modesty. It is equally about ferocious resolve, an almost stoic determination to do whatever needs to be done to make the company great. They will sell the mills or fire their brother, if that's what it takes to make the company great.

I'm not suggesting you have to fire your brother. You do, however, need to consider the example you are setting for the rest of the team if you keep your brother on staff even though he does not contribute.

The idea of ferocious resolve is intimidating to some. Does ferocious resolve require you to sacrifice the rest of your life? No. This book is about emotional intelligence and balance, not 90-hour work weeks. The whole point is to slow down, delegate and have fun. Collins says that it's possible to have a great company and a great life. He talked with a senior Gillette executive and the exec's wife about Colman Mockler, the CEO who took Gillette from good to great.

> Colman's life revolved around three great loves: his family, Harvard, and Gillette. Even during the darkest and most intense times of

the takeover crises of the 1980s and despite the increasingly global nature of Gillette's business, Mockler maintained remarkable balance in his life. He did not significantly reduce the amount of time he spent with his family, rarely working evenings or weekends. He maintained his disciplined worship practices. He continued his active work on the governing board of Harvard College...

"It really wasn't that hard for him. He was so good at assembling the right people around him, and putting the right people in the right slots, that he just didn't need to be there all hours of the day and night. That was Colman's whole secret to success and balance."

Mockler had the right people in place, those who could take the shot at the buzzer.

We can define an engaged entrepreneur as one who is fully absorbed by and enthusiastic about the business and so takes positive action to engage the employees in the vision and strategy of the business. We stated earlier that engagement is the power that animates strategic growth. The source of that power is the engaged entrepreneur, and an entrepreneur engages through leadership.

How Leadership Cascades Down through the Business

A common concern is the extent to which a leader must lead. That is, how much control or oversight must the leader exert? The answer is a little surprising. Leadership is not about control or oversight. The actual tasks or functions that constitute leadership are indirect. A wonderful allegory is found in the video "How Wolves Change Rivers," produced by Sustainable Man of San Francisco and available at sustainableman.org. Sustainable Man principal Steve Agnos told me the narration came from British writer George Monbiot's 2013 TED Talk "For More Wonder, Rewild the World."

The video is a poetic illustration of a trophic cascade. The word *trophic* relates to the food habits or feeding relationship of the organisms in a food chain. A trophic cascade is a natural phenomenon that occurs when you introduce change at the top of a food chain.

Until the 1880s Yellowstone National Park had large aspen groves. By 1883 a determined effort to eliminate gray wolves from the park was underway. The first trophic cascade began. With fewer wolves, the elk population expanded out of control, eating all the small aspen shoots and saplings. Over the course of a century, as the older trees died out they were not replaced. The result was large treeless areas of grassland.

In an effort to reverse the trophic cascade a small number of gray wolves were reintroduced to the park in 1995. The elk quickly learned to avoid the places – the valleys and gorges – where wolves could trap them. Monbiot describes the trophic cascade brought on by the wolves:

> Immediately those places started to regenerate. In some of the areas the height of the trees quintupled in just six years. Bare valley sides quickly became forests of aspen, willow and cottonwood. As soon as that happened the birds started moving in. The number of song birds, migratory birds started to increase greatly. The number of beavers started to increase because beavers like to eat the trees. And beavers are like wolves, they are eco-system engineers creating niches for other species. The dams they built provided habitats for otters, muskrats, ducks, fish, reptiles and other amphibians. The wolves killed coyotes and as a result of that the numbers of rabbits and mice increased; and as a result of that the number of hawks increased. More weasels, more foxes, more badgers.

> Here's where it gets really interesting: the wolves changed the behavior of the rivers. They began to meander less, there was less of erosion, the channels narrowed and pools formed, all of which was great for the habitat. The rivers changed in response to the wolves.

The small pack of wolves started a trophic cascade that tumbled down the food chain, resulting in a change of the physical geography of the park itself.

The trophic cascade is a natural phenomenon that's inevitable when you make changes at the top of the food chain. This is why it was so important for Colman Mockler to put the right people in place.

Another way of creating a trophic cascade is to focus on a singular goal. In 1987 Alcoa, the aluminum giant, was not doing well financially, and it was having worker safety issues. Paul O'Neill was brought in as

CEO and announced at the first investors' meeting that the new goal of the company was *safety*. That was it – just safety. No talk of profits, acquisitions or downsizing – nothing that Wall Street wanted to hear.

O'Neill's singular focus on safety proved to be a trophic cascade. No one from union bosses, to managers, to investors could criticize him for wanting "to save lives." When one worker did die, O'Neill called a meeting and announced "we are all responsible." Surely this is not what his lawyers would have advised, but the extra cost of settling the lawsuit was by far compensated by the message sent to the troops: we have to do better. And indeed they did, for the only way to really improve safety is to improve the business, production, communication, innovation – everything. The entire landscape of the company had to change. And to the delight of the investors, the positive impact on profitability and share price was dramatic.

The trophic cascade is the true power source of leadership. Changes made at the top tumble down and change the landscape. Effective leadership is in many ways the search for, and exercise of, trophic cascades.

Six Topics of the Story Map

Leading means that you work *on* the business, not *in* the business. Working on your business means you design the conceptual framework of the business. All great businesses are unique but the stories of many great ones share a common framework. That framework can be illustrated in a Story Map. The topics in the map are these:

1. Purpose
2. Vision
3. Strategy
4. Values
5. Innovation
6. Culture

The first three topics define the business and set its direction; the last three define the people in the business. You can document all of these topics – and it is a useful exercise to work through with your team – but primarily the Story Map is an oral tradition that has to be lived every business day. Before the age of printing all cultures survived by being passed down through oral tradition. This still happens today in cultures where the language is not often printed. Oral tradition defines a culture and keeps it alive.

It used to be said that we are thinking people who feel, but science has now shown us to be feeling people who think. Learning has an emotional component. Brain scans demonstrate that stories connect us. There is something in our emotional wiring that connects us to stories and to the storyteller. The best way to deliver technical information is to thread it through a story. It has been shown that information learned this way can come back to us decades later when the story is recalled.

The leader's job is to act as an elder and ensure that the oral traditions of the company are passed down to succeeding generations in the business. The tool the leader uses to do this is stories. This is what Norman Mayne, CEO of Dorothy Lane Markets, is doing in the hour or so he spends talking with new hires. By talking with these minimum-wage front-line employees Mayne is building culture through an oral tradition.

In the same way that successful outsourcing relationships do not just happen, successful employee engagement and alignment with company goals and objectives do not just happen. The elements of the Story Map cascade throughout the company, changing the grassland, rivers and topography of the business.

· · · · · · · · · · · · · · ·

The leader's job is to act as an elder and ensure that the oral traditions of the company are passed down.

· · · · · · · · · · · · · · ·

Reading the topics of the Story Map can be confusing at first because the names of the topics do not have generally accepted business definitions and are often used interchangeably. The easiest way to understand the Story Map topics is to think of them as pieces of a puzzle. The Story Map is similar to the five Ws journalists use to ensure they get the full story – who, what, where, when and why.

The Story Map is designed to reveal the fully illustrated story of the business. Working through the topics of a Story Map converts an entrepreneur's intuition into articulation. Telling is leading. Telling the story of the business and illustrating it in the Story Map make it real.

Leadership means answering these questions
through the oral tradition of the "Story Map"

**WHY ARE WE
RUNNING THIS
BUSINESS?**

 **WHERE IS THE
BUSINESS
GOING LONG TERM?**

**HOW ARE WE
GOING TO WIN?**

 **WHEN DO WE
PUT THE
BUSINESS SECOND?**

**HOW DO WE
MANAGE CHANGE?**

 **HOW DO WE BUILD
A COMMUNITY OF
TALENTED PEOPLE?**

The Story Map answers six questions:

1. Why are we running this business?
2. Where is this business going long term?
3. How are we going to win?
4. When do we put the business second?
5. How do we manage change?
6. How do we build a community of talented people?

1. Purpose

Purpose answers the question, why are we running this business?

The dictionary definition of purpose is "the reason for which something is done or created or for which something exists." As an example of the interchangeability of these terms, in his book *Managing for Results* Peter F. Drucker used the word mission instead of purpose and asked a slightly different question: "What business are we in?"

In the same sense that a railroad company should be in the transportation business, purpose should define the business in a way that meets a fundamental, permanent need. Purpose lasts for generations. People may no longer need buggy whips but they will always need a ride.

Purpose is what Jeff Bezos has in mind when he asks what will *not* change. Customers will always want better prices, faster delivery and more choice. Amazon's purpose is to create a customer-first retail experience. This purpose implicitly acknowledges that the online format may not be permanent.

Southwest Airlines doesn't tell the story of being in the airline business. Southwest is in the freedom business. Its purpose is to democratize the skies, to make air travel as available and as flexible for average Americans as it has been for the well to do. William Taylor and Polly LaBarre explain in *Mavericks at Work* that the freedom purpose infuses everything Southwest does – from advertising ("You are now free to move about the country") to messages to its 30,000-plus employees ("You are now free to be your best"). The authors conclude, "Business strategies change. Market positioning changes. But purpose does not change. Everybody at Southwest is a freedom fighter."

Every business has to figure out its higher purpose. Everyone in the business needs to know the difference they are trying to make, not just in their market but in the world.

Purpose sets you apart. Purpose appeals to a higher power. Think of Apple and its "rage against the machine" ethos. Steve Jobs's first big publicity outing, which was almost canceled by the board for fear of controversy, was its 1984 Super Bowl commercial. An Olympian with a large Olympic hammer runs down the aisle of an anonymous stadium. The stadium is filled with thousands of expressionless people with ashen faces and sunken eyes. Big Brother is droning at them through a gigantic computer monitor. The athlete swings and swings the hammer, rotating to full speed, letting it go in slow motion. The hammer crashes through the monitor, slowly showering glass as freedom reigns. Twenty years later, in 2014 the Apple story is "Gigantic, gigantic… you're more powerful than you think." The need to rage and be gigantic will not change.

A common purpose in companies that successfully hire their buyers is to build a healthy, happy community of shareholders, employees, customers and suppliers. This purpose is eternal.

2. Vision

Vision answers the question, where is this business going long term?

Vision is a mental image produced by the imagination. Having vision implies an unusual competence in discernment or perception and intelligent foresight. Vision is the long-term destination of the business. Your vision could be

- » To be the best bakery in Oakland County
- » To develop a world-class engineering firm
- » To have locations across the country
- » To grow at 15% per year for 15 years and increase our multiple to 10×
- » To build a strong company that no longer relies on the owner and provides a secure future for the employees

One of the most famous vision statements ever was made in 1961 by President Kennedy: "I believe that this nation should commit itself to achieving the goal, before this decade is out, of landing a man on the moon and returning him safely to earth." At that time there was no rocket that could land on the moon – only theories about how it might be done.

Apollo 11 was launched in July 1969. The mission was a direct result of President Kennedy's vision statement, clearly defined with a beginning and an end. That giant leap for mankind would never have happened without the trophic cascade started by President Kennedy in 1961.

In business succession the owners needs to develop a vision of what succession will look like over time. The three pillars are what activities the owner wants to be engaged in, how much money is needed and how control will be transferred. With this vision firmly in mind the owner can take decisive and positive action steps to carve it out in reality.

3. Strategy

Strategy answers the question, how are we going to win?

Strategy applies to every type of business. Many people think a company of five or six people is too small for strategy. But Jeff Bezos at Amazon – a really big company – has a "two pizza" rule. If a meeting at Amazon requires more than two pizzas, meaning more than seven or eight people, the team is too big to be effective. Small businesses *can* form effective teams and develop winning strategies.

Strategy is about choice. If the leader and employees make conscious choices about what to do – and what not to do – they are engaged in strategy. If those choices add value, the strategy has been successful.

During 2000–2009 Proctor & Gamble increased in value by $100 billion. The story is told in *Playing to Win: How Strategy Really Works* by P&G's former CEO A.G. Lafley and chief strategy consultant Roger Martin. The authors do a great job of demystifying strategy and making it accessible: "Strategy can seem mystical and mysterious. It isn't. It is easily defined. It is a set of choices about winning. It is an integrated set of choices that uniquely positions the firm in its industry so as to create sustainable advantage and superior value relative to the competition."

Lafley and Martin pose five interrelated questions. Together, the answers create strategy:

1. "What is your winning aspiration? The purpose of your enterprise, its motivating aspiration." To aspire means to direct your hopes or ambitions toward achieving something. In

choosing the term aspiration, the authors are using a term that incorporates purpose and vision, and they are adding the idea of stretching goals or reaching new heights.

2. "Where will you play? A playing field where you can achieve that aspiration." In the schoolyard we played games controlled by others in a zero-sum, win-lose environment. The teachers told us that winning was not important as long as we tried. The game of business is different in many ways. It is no fun unless you win and there is no point in simply trying. Unlike the schoolyard, you get to define the field, the rules and the referees. This is not a fierce game, it is a smart game where you choose what you're best at and how and what you can win at. Once you make these choices, you invent your own game with your own ball. And you start to play.

3. "How will you win? The way you will win on the chosen playing field." How you will win depends on your value proposition and what your customers value. You need to understand the value drivers: Price? Service? Value? Speed? Originality? These are the choices that determine how you will win.

4. "What capabilities must be in place? The set and configuration of capabilities required to win in the chosen way." Capabilities refer to business processes that deliver your value proposition to your customers. You can compare your capabilities with the four spinning plates of strategic growth that we talked about in Chapter 6: marketing, operational infrastructure, human resources and finance.

5. "What management systems are required? The systems and measures that enable the capabilities and support the choices." Management systems refer to monitoring, metrics, training and support. This also incorporates the learning and growth aspect of the corporation.

These choices and the relationships between them set the stage for a trophic cascade, with the choices at the top creating the context for the choices below them, and choices at the bottom influencing and refining those before them.

As you review these five questions it should become obvious that none of this is new or abstract. All five are basic commonsense questions. Strategy is not mystical, it's really more about organizing the concepts that we have already learned and applying them systematically.

A *Playing to Win* strategy might look like this:

© A.G. Lafley and Roger L. Martin. Reprinted with permission.

At P&G a playing-to-win strategy was developed for each product category. Lafley and Martin asked themselves, how do we win in beauty products? In garbage bags? In soap? And so on for each product.

In addition to strategies for your product or service, you should develop a playing-to-win strategy for each stakeholder in your business: owners, employees, suppliers and customers. Examples of the types of strategies you could develop for each stakeholder are as follows:

» Employee engagement
» Long-term relationships with suppliers
» A compelling value proposition for customers
» A succession plan

The first three topics of the Story Map – purpose, vision and strategy – focused on the engagement of the business. The next three – values, innovation and culture – focus on the engagement of the people in the business.

4. Values

Values answer the question, when do we put the business second?

Values are principles or standards of behavior; they're one's judgment of what is important in life.

Values, like purpose, are also permanent. Values are the limits of business. Values are where you say, "No, I won't make money that way because it goes against my values."

From a company perspective values are the reason a decision can be made that overrules logic. When Sears introduced its no-hassle return policy, it was immediately obvious that it cost money, but it also built customer loyalty, and a no-hassle return policy has become an almost universal rule of retail. This is similar to Amazon's customer-first values: when you alert a customer that they have already purchased an item, you can measure – exactly – the number of lost sales. It is impossible to measure the benefits of those lost sales.

A forensic engineer follows the lead of science. This means that the engineer applies the scientific method to investigate and answer the problems his or her clients present. Occasionally a client will be disappointed with the scientific outcome because it means they don't have a claim. They will request that the engineer ignore the science and see if they can bluff their way through. The engineer refuses to do that and knows from personal experience that it will cost him or her money. It's difficult to prove that this practice is beneficial for the engineer's business, but this engineer will have a very good reputation and lots of work.

A good example of a lack of values involves the owner of a lucrative disposal business who hauled toxic wastewater out of factories. His contract was to drive from Ontario down the I-75 and dispose of this contaminated material at a processing plant in Florida. He explained his high margins like this: after he cleared customs he would open the valve in the back of the tank just enough to create a slow leak. Twenty-four hours later, when he got to Florida, the tank would be empty, so he could return home without paying the waste-processing fee. His rationale was that in any one place only a few drops were spilled so he was doing no harm. He was the lowest bidder; his customers asked no questions.

Most people would refuse to be a part of poisoning the environment no matter how dispersed or profitable it was – it wouldn't fit with their values.

Good values act like magnetic north, pulling the right kinds of people together, providing comfort, security and reassurance that they will be safe.

5. Innovation

Innovation answers the question, how do we manage change?

Change is constant. What isn't constant is the rate of change. Eric Schmidt of Google reported in 2010 that the amount of data being created every two days was equivalent to all the data created throughout history until 2003. In 2013 some estimate it takes 10 minutes to produce the same amount. How do we cope? The answer is that we have to embrace the change and change our business and its practices with it. We change our business through innovation. The exponential rate of change is evidence of our ability to innovate.

The human quality of innovation is a specific type of imagination. Imagination is a thought or mental image that is not brought into existence. We can imagine a supernova but we can't bring it into existence.

When something is brought into existence it is called a creation. A creation may or may not have commercial value. We can sit down with our children and do finger painting that may be very creative, but it is unlikely to have commercial value.

A creation that has commercial value and can be protected by patents is called an invention. United States patent law requires that an invention meet the following criteria:

» **New or novel:** The invention must be demonstrably different from publicly available ideas, inventions or products (so-called "prior art"). This does not mean that every aspect of an invention must be novel. For example, new uses of known processes, machines and compositions of matter and materials are patentable. Incremental improvements on known processes may also be patentable.
» **Useful:** The invention must have some application or utility or be an improvement over existing products or techniques.
» **Non-obvious:** The invention cannot be obvious to a person of "ordinary skill" in the field; non-obviousness is usually demonstrated by showing that practicing the invention yields surprising, unexpected results.

By contrast, in a business an innovation is anything the business has not done before and that adds revenue, reduces cost or increases efficiency or value.

Innovation can be as simple as using a paperclip to hold two parts together or as complex as an iPhone.

Strategy itself is an example of an innovation process. The idea of playing to win is to create your own game with your own rules that create value. That's a pure innovation play.

What is the importance of innovation? PricewaterhouseCoopers published the Innovation Survey, arguing that the size and profitability of a company is no guarantee of future success. The only guarantee, they say, is innovation. In February 2007 Lehman Brothers' stock hit a record high; less than two years later the company was bankrupt. The cause could be described as innovation failure. Mortgage credit swaps were imaginative but they were toxic – they created a lot of cash but it was only a mirage of value.

The PwC Innovation Survey revealed the 10 characteristics that separate the highest innovation performers from the lowest. The number one differentiator is the trust the company placed in the people who were in charge of innovation.

Ron Joyce, cofounder of Tim Hortons, explains the benefit of innovation in his book *Always Fresh*:

> In order to succeed, a company has to continually innovate. To many outside observers, Tim Hortons may have appeared to be successful in everything the company had attempted. In fact, the company's success was built on testing and trying new products; often, ideas failed to live up to their potential or our expectations. Although it may seem counterintuitive, making mistakes in business can actually be a good thing. If you don't make mistakes, it typically means you aren't taking enough risks that will lead to continued success. Some ideas will work and some won't. A culture of innovation in a business comes hand in hand with a tolerance of failure.

We have observed that innovation is a form of creativity. Some view creativity as artistic, as something that may be unreliable. Consider movies: one year a blockbuster and the next year a flop. One studio, however, Pixar, has had an unbroken, almost unnatural string of successes. How does Pixar do this? Ed Catmull's book, *Creativity, Inc.*, answers that question. He describes how movies start as basic, almost embarrassingly simple ideas that are then worked and worked until they finally become movies.

> People tend to think of creativity as a mysterious solo act, and they typically reduce products to a single idea…

> A movie contains literally tens of thousands of ideas… Creativity must be present at every level of every artistic and technical part of the organization. The leaders sort through a mass of ideas to find the ones that fit into a coherent whole…

In *Innovation and Entrepreneurship* Peter F. Drucker tells us that innovation is rarely sparked by a "flash of genius." It is more often the product of "organized, systematic, rational work" performed by entrepreneurs who have developed the habit of seeing the world through the lens of opportunity. They refuse to be constrained by what exists at this point in time. They *feel the motion* of the business.

The Business Development Bank of Canada (BDC) advises entrepreneurs to develop an "innovation portfolio." This portfolio is an audit of all innovation initiatives and possibilities in the firm. BDC says,

> Innovation is really about responding to change in a creative way; it's about generating new ideas, conducting R&D, improving processes or revamping products and services. At another level, it's also a mindset in your business; your employees are always focused on continuous improvement and constantly thinking outside of the box.

Innovation requires a tolerance for risk, the ability to fail and an acceptance that we will fail – and that we will continuously resolve those failures.

While innovation requires a Zen-like acceptance of failure, the end result is magic. Ed Catmull discovered this basic truth while making *Toy Story*:

For 20 years, I pursued a dream of making the first computer-animated film. To be honest, after that goal was realized – when we finished *Toy Story* – I was a bit lost. But then I realized the most exciting thing I had ever done was to help create the unique environment that allowed that film to be made. My new goal became... to build a studio that had the depth, robustness, and will to keep searching for the hard truths that preserve the confluence of forces necessary to create magic.

How do you engage the magic of innovation in your business? Set aside time to discuss innovation. Ask everyone to describe one interesting innovation idea that may possibly apply in the business. Let everyone know that innovation magic requires thousands of good ideas, most of which will be discarded. Many of the best innovation companies, such as Gore-Tex and 3M, ask employees to set aside up to 15% of their work-week for unstructured innovation time.

Recognize innovation through awards and newsletters. Share the wealth, recognize the innovator as a partner sharing in the value they create. Success breeds success, engaging a cascade of innovation. Lights, camera... magic!

6. Culture

Culture answers the question, how do we build a community of talented people?

Culture is an integrated attitude and pattern of behavior shared by a particular social group. The noun is from the French *culture,* originally meaning growing or cultivating. This meaning evolved in English to include cultivation of the mind, faculties and manners.

In business we refer to the shared behaviors of the company both internally and externally as the corporate culture. Contrary to popular belief culture is not difficult to manage or change. Culture grows naturally whether we pay attention or not. Every group has a culture, good, bad or indifferent. But the inspiring part of the definition is that culture grows naturally. It can be cultivated.

Tony Hsieh opened a shoe store with a big vision that included a specific culture. Within a decade it was selling a billion dollars' worth of shoes per year. In a 2010 article in *Inc.* magazine, Hsieh describes the culture of Zappos, his online shoe retailer:

> Zappos sells shoes and apparel online, but what distinguished us from our competitors was that we'd put our company culture above all else. We'd bet that by being good to our employees – for instance, by paying for 100 percent of health care premiums, spending heavily on personal development, and giving customer service reps more freedom than at a typical call center – we would be able to offer better service than our competitors. Better service would translate into lots of repeat customers, which would mean low marketing expenses, long-term profits, and fast growth. Amazingly, it all seemed to be working.

Ed Catmull describes what is required to work with the creative types at Pixar:

> What's equally tough, of course, is getting talented people to work effectively with one another. That takes trust and respect, which we as managers can't mandate; that must be earned over time. What we can do is construct an environment that nurtures trusting and respectful relationships and unleashes everyone's creativity. If we get that right, the result is a vibrant community where talented people are loyal to one another and their collective work, everyone feels that they are part of something extraordinary, and their passion and accomplishments make the community a magnet for talented people coming out of schools or working at other places. I know what I'm describing is the antithesis of the free-agency practices that prevail in the movie industry, but that's the point: I believe that community matters.

Many of the ideas in this book – "we're great," trust, emotional intelligence, open-book management, employee engagement and transferring control – are aimed at building a culture, a value creation culture. The medium in which that culture can grow was explained in 2012 by Paul O'Neill, former CEO of Alcoa:

> I believe an organization has the potential for greatness if every person can say yes to three questions without reservation. The

first is, "Can I say every day I am treated with dignity and respect by everyone I encounter without respect to my pay grade, or my title, or my race, or ethnicity or religious beliefs or gender?" And you know, there are not a lot of places like that.

The second question is, "Am I given the things I need – education, training, tools, encouragement – so I can make a contribution to this organization that gives meaning to my life?" And the third question is, "Am I recognized for what I do by someone I care about?"

The Story Map of Hire Your Buyer

A Story Map can be quite short. This is the way Jack Ma, founder of Alibaba, the Chinese e-commerce giant, described his company's story in a letter to his 21,000 employees:

> We operate by the principle of "living seriously and working happily." We know well we haven't survived because our strategies are farsighted and brilliant, or because our execution is perfect, but because for 15 years we have persevered in our mission of "making it easier to do business across the world," because we have insisted on a "customer first" value system, because we have persisted in believing in the future, and because we have insisted that normal people can do extraordinary things.

Here is an application of the Story Map process to the hire your buyer strategy:

Purpose. The purpose of hiring your buyer is to provide owners and employees with a place of safety, financially and ethically; to provide meaningful, engaging work; and to create value, income and equity both internally for the owner and employees and externally for the suppliers and customers.

Vision. We will grow the company to 32× FMV in 15 years. By that time the owner will be completely retired and have sufficient funding to finance retirement and a legacy. A team of engaged employees will own and run a healthy, growing, vibrant company.

Strategy. We will win. We will win together. We will win by defining a game we believe in and that we can best play. We will win by defining a value proposition and competitive advantage that creates an attractive force. We will win by developing the capabilities and management systems required to allow us to play our best. We will win through strategic growth.

Values. We believe in ourselves and our people. We believe that together ordinary people can accomplish extraordinary things. We will never ask anyone to do something they do not believe in. Any employee may "pull the cord" at any time and stop the line so that we can review what we're doing. People's needs for safety, respect and appreciation always come first.

Innovation. Every aspect of the way in which we play is continuously changing. We understand that risk, opposition and paradox are the breadcrumbs left along the trail by opportunity. We will engage in Integrative Thinking to resolve and get past these opportunity paradoxes. We understand that failure is a necessary element of discovery and we accept and support each other in continuous failure. We will strive to be candid and honest in our feedback while at the same time protecting the dignity of the people with whom we communicate.

Culture. We will strive to continuously imagine a better way to interact. We will avoid hurting each other but we will also avoid allowing each other to labor under misunderstandings or pursue dead ends. We expect conflict and will resolve it simply. We will present a united front and keep business issues within the business. We will strive to be the best without sacrificing a balanced life.

Your own Story Map may include some, all or none of these elements; it may be longer or shorter – the only truly important point is that you develop your own oral tradition and your own personal stories of triumph and defeat that will connect, motivate and inspire your buyers.

In the last chapter we tie the hire your buyer information together through – you guessed it – a story.

Chapter 9

A Different Ending

THIS STORY IS A RETELLING of the first story in the book, but this version comes from my imagination. It is the story I want to bring into existence; it is the value I want to create. This time Jack receives good advice, which was not simply aimed at maximizing the amount he could borrow. What it did was alert him to the Navistar exposure so that when it went down, MarMac was not as badly damaged as it might have been and Jack was also protected in other ways.

Jack Martin turned 68 in 2006; he had owned Martin Machining Inc. (MarMac) for 33 years. Jack was a gruff old-school type but he did his best to be sociable when the occasion called for it. Although he would never tell a joke he was known to chuckle and smile occasionally.

Jack worked long hours to get his business established but he always made a point of speaking with his children before bed, even calling them if he couldn't make it home. He tried to make it to important family events even if he had to cancel the odd business meeting to do so.

Jack's oldest son, Fred, had learned to play guitar and other instruments at school. Jack had gone to some of Fred's recitals and some of the other parents said Fred was quite a good musician. At university Fred majored in music and talked about playing guitar in a band. Jack didn't like the idea of music; he felt it was not a stable way to make a living. Jack asked Fred to come into the business, hoping he would take over someday.

Fred never really took to the business. He was a reliable employee but he wasn't enthusiastic. He tried, but he made some mistakes. Jack wasn't critical but he was reluctant to give Fred responsibility until he was ready.

One day Fred came to Jack and said the business was just not for him – he had decided to do a teaching degree and become a music teacher. Jack was disappointed but he also understood that Fred was not cut out for the world of business.

Angela Barrister was a licensed insurance broker. Fifteen years earlier she had told Jack that it was very risky to have all his investments in one basket – the business. Angela explained that a private pension plan for Jack and his wife would provide security and creditor-proofing. Jack replied that his own business was his best investment. Angela politely persisted, saying that in a business there is always a risk of bankruptcy and that Jack owed it to himself and his family to speak with his accountant about a pension plan.

. . . .

This time Jack receives good valuation advice, which was not simply aimed at maximizing the amount he could borrow. What it did was alert him to the Navistar exposure.

. . . .

Jack had two concerns: the rate of return in a pension, which was only about 5% a year, and the fact that the money in the pension would be tied up and could not be used in the business. The accountant said that even though the rate of return seemed low compared with the business and even though it would tie up funds, a pension plan was a good idea because it would protect Jack if there was ever a problem with the business.

In 2006 MarMac's best sales rep, Emilio Santarosa, told Jack he had received a good offer from a competitor, QuantaTool. Emilio's wife was pregnant so he preferred to stay at MarMac rather than take a risk on an offer from QuantaTool that might not work out. Emilio wanted to buy some shares and someday take over MarMac, since Jack's son didn't seem interested.

At first Jack was upset that Emilio had spoken with a competitor. Jack's lawyer said not to worry. "Emilio has a good reputation in the industry; it's not surprising he would get an offer." The lawyer said that employee ownership could be a good thing. He agreed with Jack that a sales rep would not have the technical skills to run the company, but he pointed out that Jack could build a team with all the skills needed to run the company.

Jack said he had heard about "golden handcuff" agreements: the employee gets shares but will lose those shares if they leave the company. The employee has to have "skin in the game," meaning real money to buy the shares.

"It's your decision," the lawyer advised, "but the best way to build a long-term relationship is through trust. There are no guarantees but the probabilities are higher." Trust had to start with Jack: no golden handcuffs, no worry about skin in the game. The lawyer explained that Jack could develop a succession strategy in which the employees would add *skill* in the game.

"The trick," said the lawyer, "is that the employees start with the business platform you have created. This gives them a 15-year head start over where they would be if they started their own business. What they are really doing is taking it to the next level."

A business valuator said MarMac could be worth $5 million. But the value was discounted by half because the business depended so heavily on Jack's continuous involvement. In addition, the top customer, Navistar, accounted for 50% of the business – but Jack had never allowed that percentage to be greater. Still, what would happen if Jack couldn't come to work or Navistar stopped sending orders? These were troubling questions.

Jack realized he had a problem but he had no idea what to do. He didn't want to sell MarMac, at least not yet, and he certainly was not happy with the big discount the valuator put on the business. He had always wanted to be able to get $5 million for his business and that was what it should have been worth.

. . . .

The trick is that the employees start with the business platform you have created. This gives them a 15-year head start.

. . . .

Jack met with both his accountant and his lawyer. They agreed it was a complicated decision. There was no single correct answer or approach. They advised Jack that he needed to resolve three key questions:

» What would his activity be during the transition?
» How and when would he transfer control?
» What income and equity did he require to finance his lifestyle in retirement?

ACTIVITY   CONTROL   INCOME

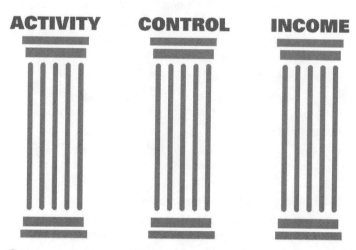

Once we know when and where these pillars will be in the ground, we can reverse engineer to start building them today.

Jack had to decide what his own continuing role in the business was going to be. Did he want to continue full time? For how long? Was he interested in some part-time work after the transition? What did he really like about his work? What did he find irritating? Based on these criteria Jack could write his own game plan for his life with the business.

Transferring control meant that Jack had to face the inevitable: at some point he would no longer have control. The lawyer explained that there were two types of control: control of work activities and legal control.

Relinquishing control of work activities meant that Jack needed to delegate. As the valuator stated, "delegation equals value." Delegating required Jack and the team to develop a common understanding of goals and objectives. Once agreed it was up to each employee to take responsibility for accomplishing those objectives. This step could be painful because Jack would need to recognize that some of his employees may not thrive in this type of environment.

Voting control meant final authority. Retaining legal control meant that if the team decided on something Jack didn't agree with, he could veto it. The lawyer advised Jack not to give up final authority until the succession plan was deeply embedded and working well. Jack could retain voting control for another five to 10 years, until the employees passed a 50% ownership stake. During this time Jack had to learn to manage in such a way that it would not be necessary to use his final authority. The better he was able to manage without using final authority, the less concern he would have when he finally did turn over voting control to the employees.

The final issue was income and equity. This issue was based solely on how much money Jack needed to get out of the business to meet the lifestyle needs of his family. The accountant advised Jack to go back to Angela Barrister and work out a personal financial plan.

After calculating all lifestyle expenses and other requirements Angela told Jack that his goal of $5 million was a little more than he would need to meet his lifestyle objectives, but it was always a good idea to have a buffer. Jack was concerned about providing a decent legacy for his children, who would not be involved in the business, and for his grandchildren. He was also concerned about ensuring that the tax bills arising on his death could be paid. Angela recommended permanent life insurance as the least expensive option; the accountant agreed.

The plan was to sell MarMac to the key employees. Jack had confidence in Emilio as far as sales went – Emilio was responsible for all sales with the exception of the Navistar account. If Emilio left to work with a competitor the potential loss of sales if his accounts followed him would put a significant dent in MarMac's value. This would leave it even more vulnerable to the possible loss of Navistar's business.

Jack's production manager was close to retirement so Jack was concerned about the technical and production side of the business. Emilio told Jack that the reason he had talked to the owners of QuantaTool was that he had a good friend who was the production manager there. Emilio was confident that together the two of them could manage the business. As it turned out QuantaTool had lost its longtime sales manager and that was why they made an offer to Emilio. Emilio also told Jack that the production manager had approached the owner of QuantaTool about acquiring some equity shares in the company but the owner kept postponing the discussion.

Jack developed a basic plan with the lawyer and accountant. The accountant said that the final tax structure – an ESOP, consulting fees paid to Jack, trusts, holding companies, etc. – would be finalized after the value creation plan was developed. For the plan to work the key employees had to see that the value of MarMac would increase enough to make it worth their while. It had to be win-win.

The plan was designed to work over a 10-year period, from 2007 to 2016. By that time Jack would be 79. The plan was broken up into two five-year periods.

In the first five-year period, 2007–11, Jack would slow down and progressively delegate control. MarMac would pay Jack $100,000 up front and $40,000 per month for 60 months, for a total of $2.5 million, which was the fair market value of the company in 2007. During this period the key employees would get bonuses over their base salaries in every month that MarMac made the payment to Jack.

In addition to the bonus, the key employees would get an option to buy 50% of the shares of MarMac for $1.00 in total at the end of the first five years. This option had two conditions: first, all the payments had to be made to Jack during the first five years, and second, the key employees had to agree to pay full FMV for the remaining 50% of the shares over the second five-year period.

The plan was that MarMac would double in value over the first five years, to $5 million, so that 50% of the shares in 2011 would be worth $2.5 million. If this worked, which seemed feasible, Jack would get $5 million in total, plus consulting fees along the way for the work he chose to do.

Emilio couldn't quite believe what he was hearing. "So we're getting half the company for free?"

"Not really," said Jack. "You don't have to put out any money personally but you do have to earn it and you have to ensure that my family and the rest of the employees are well taken care of. Go talk to that production manager and see what he thinks." Within a month, MarMac had a new production manager.

During the second half of 2007 and into 2008 Jack's larger customers started taking longer to pay, from 60 days to 120 days. The bank called Jack about an extension on his line of credit to $1.5 million. The bank also asked for a personal guarantee and a mortgage on Jack's home, where he had lived with his wife for more than 30 years. His home was worth $400,000, it was fully paid off and it was the only asset Jack held outside of his business.

Jack was 70 years old by this time, he had been operating his business for almost 35 years; he had seen bad times before. But this time his accountant told him to be careful. Banks were ruthless and they would go after his home if there were problems. Jack met with Emilio and he agreed that it was not a good idea to extend the line of credit. Emilio had friends on the line at Navistar and the rumors were not good. It was time to start phasing out dependence on Navistar's business.

In 2009 Navistar closed its plant and overnight MarMac lost 30% of its business and $500,000 of receivables. Jack met with Emilio and they agreed that Emilio would put up $100,000 and Jack $400,000 to keep MarMac afloat. MarMac did not make any payments to Jack in 2009 and no bonuses were paid. It was a tough period, but by reducing the hours of all employees MarMac was able to keep its best employees and its long-term customers.

Jack was concerned that MarMac may go bankrupt but Angela Barrister told him that his individual pension plan was protected even if he personally went bankrupt and that it would pay out $50,000 a year each to him and his wife for the rest of their lives. This gave Jack a lot of confidence.

The seriousness of the situation really sunk in the day Jack read in the paper that QuantaTool had declared bankruptcy.

In 2010 the economy started to turn. Jack decided to extend the original five-year plan for one year, to 2012, because 2009 was essentially a non-year as far as the plan went. With fewer competitors MarMac emerged stronger; it was able to replace the Navistar business and more. The employees were starting to get regular overtime and MarMac was thinking about hiring again. By the end of 2012 MarMac was able to catch up on the payments to Jack and had started to repay the loans to Jack and Emilio.

At the 2012 MarMac Christmas party Jack announced his retirement and the sale of the company to the key employees. Emilio and a number of the employees gave warm speeches.

Jack's son Fred spoke last. He expressed his admiration for Jack's determination in the company, but more importantly he said, "Dad didn't always appreciate my preference for music but he didn't stop me. He always supported me, and now I run the music department at Meadow Lakes High. Dad is enjoying his duties as a grandfather and surprisingly enough seems to be a fairly good assistant coach for my twin daughters' under-7 soccer team. Although I am not sure how long he will be able to keep up with those girls running up and down the field." Jack smiled and laughed.

Appendix

Seven Steps for Determining Business Value

THESE SEVEN STEPS will give you a rough idea of the type of process a buyer may go through in looking at the value of your business. This exercise also allows you to get a starting point for the value of your own business. It is not as accurate as a true valuation but it is great for the purposes of determining whether you are anywhere close to where you need to be, or want to be, for sale purposes.

This section requires information from your financial statements and reasonable estimates of certain expenses. It may be useful to review it with your accountant.

Step 1. Earnings. The starting point is to determine earnings. Earnings is a simpler idea than profit, which may require adjustments. Earnings is gross sales less cost of goods sold and expenses.

Free cash flow is determined by starting with the average of earnings over a three- or five-year timeframe and then making two further adjustments to those earnings. The adjustments are EBITDA and normalization.

Step 2. EBITDA stands for earnings before interest, taxes, depreciation and amortization. The idea is that interest, taxes, depreciation and amortization are not operational expenses that affect the business.

EBITDA is commonly used but not everyone agrees with it. Some prefer another formula called EBIT. More sophisticated valuations use DCF models. The point is that there are other methods of determining value, but they are all hypothetical, so for illustration purposes EBITDA is just fine.

Step 3. Normalization. Normalization is a process that accounts for the personal benefits that an owner of a family business takes and any other non-business lifestyle-related decisions that creep into the financial statements. Owners often pay themselves and family members salaries and benefits that are more favorable than normal salaries and may take other perks that an unrelated employee would not get. The theory is that a normal business would not pay for these additional perks so they can be added back to determine a more realistic picture of a normal free cash flow. Another common add-back is any non-recurring charges like a substantial repair or an unusual loss due to weather.

Step 4. Multiple. The multiple is determined by the return on investment that the buyer wants. To determine ROI you divide 100% by the multiple. If the multiple is 4× that means the buyer wants a 25% return on the investment per year (100% ÷ 4 = 25%). In other words, the buyer wants to make their money back in four years. Most businesses listed on BizBuySell have a multiple of between 1× and 4×.

To calculate the multiple in general terms look at the number of risk factors the business faces. The good news is that reducing the risk in your business increases the value. And here's a happy coincidence: delegation equals value. The less the business relies on the owner the more valuable it is. This means you can slow down and increase value at the same time.

It is important to note that any one of the risks in a business may be so serious that it alone may prevent a sale. For instance, if all the goodwill in the business was non-transferable personal goodwill then the only sale possible would be a liquidation sale.

Many industries rely on a rule of thumb whereby all businesses are valued using the same multiple. For example, insurance agencies are sold on the basis of 2× annual revenue. One valuator has said that rules of thumb are "dumb" because one size does not fit all. Most buyers prefer a more in-depth analysis of the risk factors of the individual business they are purchasing.

Step 5. Redundant Assets. An asset is redundant if it could be removed from the business without harming operations. Examples are fully owned real estate that could be rented out and excess cash in the bank that does not get reduced at some point during the year or seems excessive when compared with peer companies. Redundant assets represent value over and above business value that can be extracted without harming the business.

Step 6. Business Value. Business value, which is the value of the whole enterprise, equals free cash flow times a multiple plus redundant assets.

Step 7. Shareholder Value. Shareholder value is different from business value because what we are concerned about with shareholder value is the amount you will get for your shares if you sell them. The first step is to reduce business value by the amount of debt that will have to be paid or assumed on the sale of the enterprise and then calculate based on the percentage of shares you own.

What follows is a chart for getting a rough idea of the sale value of your business. If you do plan to sell your business you should seek professional assistance. This chart does not take into account the possibility of a strategic purchaser, who may pay double or more the amount calculated by this formula.

Applying the Seven-Step Formula

Step 1. Determine Earnings

Annual revenue	
Less cost of goods	
Less expenses	
Equals Earnings (average over 3 or 5 years)	

Step 2. Determine EBITDA

Earnings	
Plus interest	
Plus taxes	
Plus depreciation	
Plus amortization	
Equals EBITDA	

Step 3. Normalize Earnings to Determine Free Cash Flow

EBITDA	
Plus owner's salary and benefits above what would be paid to an outsider	
Plus family member salaries and benefits above what would be paid to an outsider	
Plus owner's family automobile expense above what would be paid to an outsider	
Plus charitable donations	
Plus or minus rent adjustment to FMV	
Plus owner's family life and disability insurance payments above what would be paid to an outsider	
Plus legal, accounting and tax advice expenses	
Plus owner retirement plan contributions	
Plus owner travel and entertainment expenses above what would be paid to an outsider	
Plus subscriptions, memberships, private clubs, etc., unless necessary to stay with business	
Plus extraordinary one-time (non-recurring) expenses	
Less annual earnings from redundant assets	
Equals Free Cash Flow (sometimes called normalized earnings)	

Step 4. Determine a Multiple

Assign a value from 1 (lowest) to 4 (highest) to each item	Value 1 to 4
Owner involvement: Does the business have a good process in place that does not require the owner (4) or do you run the business out of your head (1)?	
Goodwill: Is the goodwill in the business transferable (4) or is it the personal goodwill of the owner (1)?	
Replaceability: Can the suppliers and employees be replaced (4) or does the business depend on certain key suppliers and employees (1)?	
Financial records: Does your business have audited financial statements that reflect all income (4) or are your records informal and not inclusive of all your business revenue (1)?	
Legal documentation: Are your key agreements and legal assets documented (4) or is everything based on handshakes and personal understandings with the owner (1)?	
Clientele: Do you have a broad base of profitable clients, with no client representing more than 5% of your revenue, and do you have good customer lists and contracts (4) or do a few customers account for most sales, without customer lists or strong, transferable contracts (1)?	
Products: Does your business offer distinctly different, better and difficult-to-copy products and services; serve an exclusive territory; or offer an exclusive product line under transferable contracts or arrangements (4) or does it offer products identical to those offered by other businesses in your market area with no distinct competitive advantage (1)?	
Recurring revenue: Does your business sell via subscriptions, monthly fees, automatic delivery programs or other approaches that deliver ongoing revenue from established customers (4) or are most sales single-time transactions by one-time or occasional customers (1)?	

Assign a value from 1 (lowest) to 4 (highest) to each item	Value 1 to 4
Staffing: Does your business have key staff with transferable contracts who will assist with the business transition (4) or are you the one-and-only key person (1)?	
Location: If your business's success relies on its location, is it in a growing and desirable market area and does it have a long-term, transferable lease and good facilities and equipment (4) or will a new owner need to move or improve the location (1)?	
Brand and reputation: Does your business have a well-known name, respected reputation and top position within its competitive arena (4) or are the reputations of competitors considered stronger and preferable (1)?	
Annual sales: over $3 million (4), $1–$3 million (3), $100,000–$1 million (2), under $100,000 (1)	
Annual growth: over 15% (4), 5–15% (3), under 5% (2), 0% (1)	
Total	
Multiple: Total divided by 13	

Step 5. Evaluate Redundant Assets

Cash not required for operations	
Real estate that could be rented	
Any other assets not required in business	
Total Redundant Assets	

Step 6. Calculate Business Value

Free cash flow	
Times multiple	
Plus redundant assets	
Equals Business Value	

Step 7. Calculate Shareholder Value

Business value	
Less debt or obligations	
Divided by share ownership %	
Equals Shareholder Value	

Bibliography

Beaton, Eleanor. "The Lure of ESOPs." *Profit*, June 31, 2007.

Beatty, Carol A., and Harvey Schacter. *Employee Ownership: The New Source of Competitive Advantage.* Etobicoke, ON: John Wiley & Sons Canada, 2002.

Bezos, Jeff. "Fireside Chat with Jeff Bezos and Werner Vogels." Amazon Web Services re:Invent Conference, Nov. 2012.

Boyd, John. *Conversations on Our First 50 Years.* Golder Associates, 2011.

Brown, Peter B. "The Entrepreneurial Paradox: What Got You Into Business Isn't the Best Way to Be Successful," *Forbes,* June 23, 2013.

Burchell, Michael, and Jennifer Robin. *The Great Workplace: How to Build It, How to Keep It, and Why It Matters.* San Francisco, CA: Jossey-Bass, 2011.

Canada Life. Participating Life Insurance Financial Facts. 2012. http://www.canadalife.com/003/Home/Products/LifeInsurance/ PermanentInsurance/ParticipatingLifeInsurance/Documents/ S5_009944.

Catmull, Ed, with Amy Wallace. *Creativity, Inc.: Overcoming the Unseen Forces That Stand in the Way of True Inspiration.* New York: Random House, 2014.

Collins, Jim. *Good to Great: Why Some Companies Make the Leap... and Others Don't.* New York: HarperCollins, 2001.

Covey, Stephen M.R. *The Speed of Trust: The One Thing That Changes Everything.* New York: Free Press, 2006.

Covey, Stephen R. *7 Habits of Highly Effective People.* New York: Simon & Schuster, 1989.

Damodaran, Aswath. "Valuing Luxury." L2 Innovation Forum, Nov. 5, 2010.

Deans, Thomas William. *Every Family's Business: 12 Common Sense Questions to Protect Your Wealth,* 2nd edition. Orangeville, ON: Détente Financial Press, 2009.

Deans, Thomas William. *Willing Wisdom: 7 Questions Successful Families Ask.* Orangeville, ON: Détente Financial Press, 2013.

Deming, W. Edwards. *Out of the Crisis.* Cambridge, MA: MIT Press, 2000.

DeSteno, David. "Who Can You Trust?" *Harvard Business Review,* Mar. 2014.

Dini, John F. *Beating the Boomer Bust.* Kindle, 2012.

Drucker, Peter F. *Managing for Results.* Harper & Row, 1964.

Fenn, Donna. *Alpha Dogs: How Your Small Business Can Become a Leader of the Pack.* New York: Harper Business, 2007.

Foot, David K., with Daniel Stoffman. *Boom, Bust and Echo: Profiting from the Demographic Shift in the 21st Century.* Stoddart, 2000.

Garvin, David A. "How Google Sold Its Engineers on Management." *Harvard Business Review,* Dec. 2013.

Gerber, Michael E. *The E-Myth Revisited: Why Most Small Businesses Don't Work and What to Do About It.* New York: Harper Business, 1995.

Goleman, Daniel. "What Makes a Leader?" *Harvard Business Review,* Jan. 2014.

Hams, Brad. *Ownership Thinking: How to End Entitlement and Create a Culture of Accountability, Purpose, and Profit.* New York: McGraw-Hill, 2012.

Hsieh, Tony. "Why I Sold Zappos." *Inc. Magazine,* June 1, 2010.

Joyce, Ron. *Always Fresh: The Untold Story of Tim Hortons.* Toronto: HarperCollins, 2006.

Lafley, A.G., and Roger L. Martin. *Playing to Win: How Strategy Really Works.* Boston, MA: Harvard Business Review Press, 2013.

Lederach, John Paul. *The Moral Imagination: The Art and Soul of Building Peace.* New York: Oxford University Press, 2005.

Logan, Dave, John King and Halee Fischer-Wright. *Tribal Leadership: Leveraging Natural Groups to Build a Thriving Organization.* New York: Harper Business, 2008.

Ma, Jack. "'Unparalleled Ruthlessness' Awaits: Jack Ma's Letter to Alibaba Employees." *Wall Street Journal*, May 7, 2014.

McFarland, Keith R. *The Breakthrough Company: How Everyday Companies Become Extraordinary Performers*. New York: Crown Business, 2008.

Merfeld, Eugene, Gary Schine and David Annis. *Strategic Acquisition: A Smarter Way to Grow a Small or Medium Size Company*. Lulu, 2009.

National Center for Employee Ownership. "Research on Employee Ownership, Corporate Performance and Employee Compensation." http://www.nceo.org/articles/research-employee-ownership-corporate-performance.

Reynolds, Rod. "How to Save the Family Business." Chartered Accountants of British Columbia *Beyond Numbers*, May 2002.

Root, Randal. "Creating a Company of 'Owners.'" White paper. Rootinc.com, Oct. 23, 2012.

Rosen, Corey, and Michael Quarrey. "How Well Is Employee Ownership Working?" *Harvard Business Review*, Sept.–Oct., 1987.

Roth, Mark. "'Habitual Excellence': The Workplace According to Paul O'Neill." *Pittsburgh Post-Gazette*, May 13, 2012. http://www.post-gazette.com/business/businessnews/2012/05/13/Habitual-excellence-The-workplace-according-to-Paul-O-Neill/stories/201205130249

Sahlman, William A. "How to Write a Great Business Plan." *Harvard Business Review*, July 1997.

Sanger, David E. "VisiCalc Lawsuit Is Settled." *New York Times*, Sept. 18, 1984.

Slee, Robert T. *Midas Moments* Newsletter, Feb. 2014.

Slee, Robert T. *Private Capital Markets: Valuation, Capitalization, and Transfer of Private Business Interests*. Hoboken, NJ: John Wiley & Sons, 2011.

Sullivan, Dan. "How to Turn Your Vision into Reality." The Strategy Circle. YouTube, Oct. 29, 2012.

Tal, Benjamin. "Inadequate Business Succession Planning – A Growing Macroeconomic Risk." CIBC World Markets *In Focus*, Nov. 2012.

Taylor, William C., and Polly G. LaBarre. *Mavericks at Work: Why the Most Original Minds in Business Win*. William Morrow, 2006.

Warrillow, John. "How to Find Out What Your Business Is Really Worth." *Inc.* magazine, Oct. 4, 2010.

Wasserman, Noam. "How Founder Control Holds Back Start-ups." *Harvard Business Review* Blog Network, Apr. 11, 2014.

Willcocks, Leslie P., and Sara Cullen. "The Outsourcing Enterprise: The Power of Relationships." White paper. London: Logica/London School of Economics, 2007.

Zook, Chris, with James Allen. *Profit from the Core. Growth Strategy in an Era of Turbulence.* Boston, MA: Bain & Co., 2001.

Web Resources

BizBuySell.com
BizEquity.com
CorporateValue.net
Divestopedia.com
HBR.org (free blog subscription)
ShannonPratt.com
SuccessionTaxCounsel.com
TheSellabilityScore.com
LinkedIn Groups:
    Business Succession Professionals
    Business Valuation and Advisory Network
    Canadian Wealth and Estate Planning
    Purposeful Planning Institute

Further Reading

Beauregard, Jack. *Finding Your New Owner: For Your Business, for Your Life.* Cambridge, MA: STPI Press, 2001.

Campbell, Ian R., and H. Christopher Nobes. *50 Hurdles: Business Transition Simplified.* Mississauga, ON: Transitus Publishing, 2014.

Erickson, Tamara J. *Retire Retirement: Career Strategies for the Boomer Generation.* Boston, MA: Harvard Business School Publishing, 2008.

Franzetta, David, and Moss A. Jackson. *Changing Places: Making a Success of Succession Planning for Entrepreneurs and Family Business Owners.* Bloomington, IN: AuthorHouse, 2012.

Gadiesh, Orit, and Hugh MacArthur. *Lessons from Private Equity Any Company Can Use.* Boston: Harvard Business Press, 2008.

Hoffman, Reid, and Ben Casnocha. *The Start-up of You: Adapt to the Future, Invest in Yourself, and Transform Your Career.* New York: Crown Business, 2012.

Hughes, James E., Jr. *Family Wealth: Keeping It in the Family. How Family Members and Their Advisers Preserve Human, Intellectual, and Financial Assets for Generations,* 2nd revised edition. Princeton, NJ: Bloomberg, 2004.

Hughes, James E., Susan E. Massenzio and Keith Whitaker. *The Cycle of the Gift: Family Wealth and Wisdom.* Princeton, NJ: Bloomberg, 2012.

Johnson, Howard E. *Building Value in Your Company.* Toronto: Canadian Institute of Chartered Accountants, 2011.

Johnson, Howard E. *Selling Your Private Company.* Toronto: Canadian Institute of Chartered Accountants, 2005.

Kells, Greg. *Insider Tips on Buying a Business in Canada.* Ottawa: Sunbelt Business Brokers Canada, 2013.

Leonetti, John M. *Exiting Your Business, Protecting Your Wealth: A Strategic Guide for Owners and Their Advisors.* Hoboken, NJ/Toronto: John Wiley & Sons, 2008.

Louis, David, Samantha Prasad and Michael Goldberg. *Tax and Family Business Succession Planning,* 3rd edition. Toronto: CCH Canadian, 2009.

Mahaffy, A. Paul. *Business Succession Guide,* 3rd edition. Toronto: Carswell, 2013.

Mellen, Chris M., and Frank C. Evans. *Valuation for M&A: Building Value in Private Companies,* 2nd edition. Hoboken, NJ/Toronto: John Wiley & Sons, 2010.

Minor, Ned. *Deciding to Sell Your Business: The Key to Wealth and Freedom.* Deciding to Sell LLC, 2005.

Phillips, Perry. *Employee Share Ownership Plans: How to Design and Implement an ESOP in Canada.* Toronto: John Wiley & Sons, 2001.

Rosenfarb, Noah B. *Exit: Healthy, Wealthy and Wise – A Step-By-Step Guide to Conquering Business, Personal, Family and Financial Issues When Selling or Transferring a Business.* San Diego: Better Life Books, 2013.

Scarratt, Malcolm, and James W. Kraft. *The Advisor's Guide to Business Succession Planning,* 4th edition. Toronto: CCH Canadian, 2010.

Schenck, Barbara Findlay and John Davies. *Selling Your Business for Dummies*. Hoboken, NJ/Toronto: John Wiley & Sons, 2009.

Trottier, Richard M. *Middle Market Strategies: How Private Companies Use the Markets to Create Value*. Hoboken, NJ/Toronto: John Wiley & Sons, 2009.

Vanwyck, Wayne. *The Business Transition Crisis: Plan Your Succession Now to Beat the Biggest Business Selloff in History*. Toronto/New York: BPS Books, 2010.

Warrillow, John. *Built to Sell: Creating a Business That Can Thrive Without You*. New York: Portfolio/Penguin, 2011.

Willis, Thayer Cheatham. *Navigating the Dark Side of Wealth: A Life Guide for Inheritors*. Portland, OR: New Concord Press, 2003.

Wise, Richard M., Shannon P. Pratt and Jay E. Fishman. *Guide to Canadian Business Valuations*, 3 vols. Toronto: Carswell (loose leaf service), 1993.

About the Author

I AM AN AUTHOR, public speaker and business succession consultant.

I did not intend to be a lawyer, I intended to be in business. I read dozens of books on business. One of them was J. Paul Getty's *How to Be a Successful Executive.* Getty said that being in business was about solving problems and that your business would go as far as your ability to solve those problems. Today we describe this as change and the need for innovation.

This meant that training for business should be about learning to solve problems – every kind of problem. To learn to solve every kind of problem you needed to learn about everything (or at least try). Getty recommended law school rather than business school because he said law school was about everything, whereas business school was too narrowly focused.

In writing this book I researched and wrote a story about how badly J. Paul treated his own sons in business, driving one of them to suicide. I didn't know this story when I read his book and set the path for my life. It is interesting to consider whether I might have done things differently had I known. But in his defense, J. Paul lived before the social consciousness movement of the 1960s – in his time, abstract ideals like "the business is the priority" still reigned. Fortunately, we have learned better ways. We can manage loving relationships and build a business at the same time.

After graduation, I started my own law practice. I was attracted to corporate/tax litigation because of its complexity and the deep, intimate knowledge you have to gain about your clients and their situations. Complex corporate/tax litigation also involves teams of professionals: accountants, valuators, brokers and more. One aspect I enjoyed was the uniquely deep and respectful relationships that can form among those fighting together in the battle for justice.

Over time I migrated to tax law and in 2002 I obtained a master of laws degree in international tax. More than 30 years after finishing Getty's book and with 25 years of tax planning, business law and litigation problem-solving under my belt, I turned my attention to business succession planning. Why succession planning? Because it's about everything, so it's well suited to my skill set. Moreover, effective succession planning involves a similar deep knowledge of each client, as well as the assembling of professional teams driven by the satisfaction of a job well done.

Thank You for Reading

The essence of *Hire Your Buyer* is building community. If you would like to extend the community and discuss the ideas in the book please call me at (519) 973-1223, or email me at john@johnmilltax.com. It would be great to hear from you. You can also consider connecting on LinkedIn; and, if you are a professional, consider joining my group on LinkedIn called "Business Succession Professionals." You can also find a wealth of resources and related articles on my blog www.succession taxcounsel.com.

If you believe this book would be helpful for others then the best way to help get it out there is to post a review at Amazon. You can post reviews or buy more copies of the book by clicking on www.hireyourbuyer.com, which will take you directly to the Amazon book page.

We invite you to share your thoughts and reactions

Made in the USA
Charleston, SC
14 October 2014